J

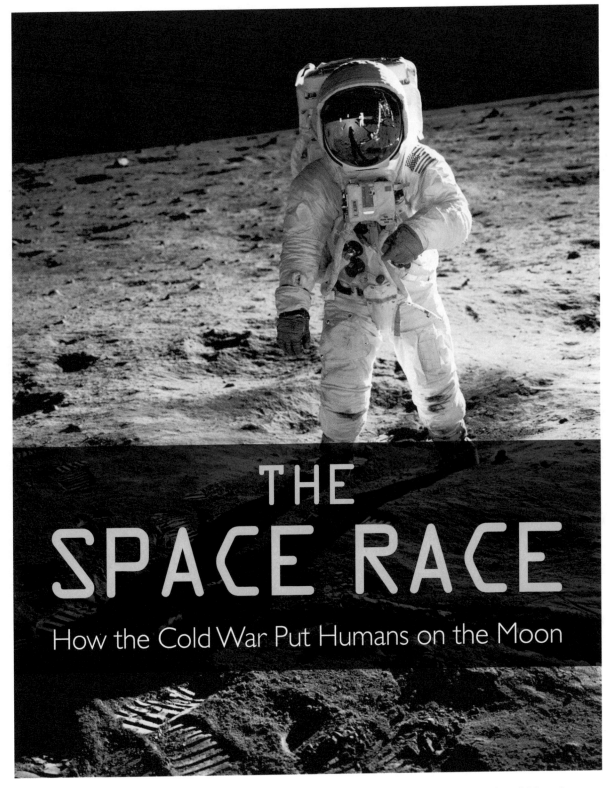

THE
SPACE RACE

How the Cold War Put Humans on the Moon

Matthew Brenden Wood

Illustrated by Sam Carbaugh

Nomad Press
A division of Nomad Communications
10 9 8 7 6 5 4 3 2 1

This book was manufactured by Versa Press
East Peoria, Illinois
May 2018, Job # J17-12585

ISBN Softcover: 978-1-61930-663-9
ISBN Hardcover: 978-1-61930-661-5

Educational Consultant, Marla Conn

Questions regarding the ordering of this book should be addressed to
Nomad Press
2456 Christian St.
White River Junction, VT 05001
www.nomadpress.net

Printed in the United States.

Titles in the Inquire & Investigate
Great Events of the Twentieth Century set

INQUIRE & INVESTIGATE

GLOBALIZATION
WHY WE CARE ABOUT FARAWAY EVENTS

Carla Mooney
Illustrated by Sam Carbaugh

INQUIRE & INVESTIGATE

THE VIETNAM WAR

Barbara Diggs
Illustrated by Sam Carbaugh

INQUIRE & INVESTIGATE

WORLD WAR II
From the Rise of the Nazi Party to the Dropping of the Atomic Bomb

Diane C. Taylor
Illustrated by Sam Carbaugh

INQUIRE & INVESTIGATE

THE SPACE RACE
How the Cold War Put Humans on the Moon

Matthew Brenden Wood
Illustrated by Sam Carbaugh

Check out more titles at www.nomadpress.net

Interested in primary sources? Look for this icon. **PS**

You can use a smartphone or tablet app to scan the QR codes and explore more! Cover up neighboring QR codes to make sure you're scanning the right one. You can find a list of URLs on the Resources page.

If the QR code doesn't work, try searching the internet with the Keyword Prompts to find other helpful sources.

🔎 Space Race

What are source notes?

In this book, you'll find small numbers at the end of some paragraphs. These numbers indicate that you can find source notes for that section in the back of the book. Source notes tell readers where the writer got their information. This might be a news article, a book, or another kind of media. Source notes are a way to know that what you are reading is true information that other people have verified. They can also lead you to more places where you can explore a topic that you're curious about!

Contents

TIMELINE

March 8, 1917 .... The Russian Revolution begins.

December 28, 1922 ..... The Union of Soviet Socialist Republics (USSR), also called the Soviet Union, is founded with Vladimir Lenin as its leader.

January 21, 1924 .... Vladimir Lenin dies.

March 16, 1926 .... Robert Goddard launches the first liquid-fueled rocket.

1929 .... Joseph Stalin becomes the leader of Soviet Union.

May 26, 1938 .... The House Un-American Activities Committee is founded.

September 1, 1939 ..... Germany invades Poland, starting World War II.

June 22, 1941 .... Adolf Hitler breaks the non-aggression pact with the USSR and the Soviets join the Allied powers.

December 7, 1941 .... Japan attacks the U.S. naval base at Pearl Harbor, Hawaii, triggering the United States' entry into World War II.

September 8, 1944 ..... The first German V-2 ballistic missile hits London, England, killing three people.

May 7, 1945 .... Germany surrenders to the Allies.

TIMELINE

August 6, 1945............ The United States drops an atomic bomb on the Japanese cities of Hiroshima and, three days later, Nagasaki.

September 2, 1945...... Japan surrenders, ending World War II.

September 29, 1945.... Wernher von Braun arrives in the United States.

April 16, 1946............. The United States sees its first successful flight of a captured V-2 rocket.

October 20, 1947 .... The USSR sees its first successful flight of a captured V-2 rocket.

June 11, 1948.............. Albert 1, a rhesus monkey, becomes the first animal to reach space on a U.S.-launched V-2.

June 24, 1948.............. The Soviet blockade of West Berlin begins.

April 4, 1949............... The North Atlantic Treaty Organization (NATO) is founded.

February 9, 1950......... U.S. Senator Joseph McCarthy claims he has knowledge of communists in the U.S. government.

June 25, 1950.............. The Korean War begins.

March 5, 1953 .... Joseph Stalin dies.

July 27, 1953............... The Korean War ends with a truce.

September 12, 1953.... Nikita Khrushchev becomes leader of the Soviet Union.

May 14, 1955............... The Warsaw Pact is founded.

August 21, 1957......... The first intercontinental ballistic missile, the R-7, is tested by the USSR.

October 4, 1957 .... *Sputnik 1*, the world's first artificial satellite, is launched by the USSR.

November 3, 1957....... The USSR launches Laika the dog, who becomes the first animal to reach orbit.

TIMELINE

January 31, 1958........ The United States launches its first satellite, *Explorer 1*.

July 29, 1958.............. The National Aeronautics and Space Administration (NASA) is formed.

February 17, 1959....... The United States launches the world's first weather satellite, *Vanguard 2*.

May 28, 1959.............. Able and Baker become the first primates to reach space.

October 7, 1959.......... The Soviet Union's *Lunar 3* sends back the first pictures of the far side of the moon.

May 1, 1960................. The USSR shoots down an American U-2 spyplane, capturing pilot Gary Powers.

July 5, 1960................. The United States launches the world's first spy satellite.

April 12, 1961.............. Soviet Yuri Gagarin becomes the first human in space.

April 17, 1961.............. The Bay of Pigs invasion fails.

May 5, 1961................. Alan Shepard becomes the first American in space.

May 25, 1961.............. U.S. President John F. Kennedy gives a speech announcing U.S. plans to land on the moon.

February 20, 1962....... John Glenn becomes the first American to orbit the earth.

October 16, 1962........ The Cuban missile crisis begins.

June 16, 1963............. Soviet Valentina Tereshkova becomes the first woman in space.

August 5, 1963........... The United States and the Soviet Union sign the Limited Nuclear Test Ban Treaty.

November 22, 1963 .... President John F. Kennedy is assassinated.

October 12, 1964 .... The USSR launches the first multi-person crew aboard *Voskhod 1*.

February 9, 1965........ The first U.S. combat troops are sent to Vietnam.

March 18, 1965 .... Soviet Alexey Leonov performs the first spacewalk.

March 23, 1965 .... The United States sends its first manned *Gemini* flight.

June 3, 1965............... Ed White performs the first American spacewalk.

January 14, 1966........ Sergei Korolev, the chief designer of the Soviet Union's space program, dies.

February 3, 1966........ The USSR's *Luna 9* makes the first soft landing on the moon.

March 16, 1966 .... America's *Gemini 8* makes the first docking in space.

June 2, 1966............... America's *Surveyor 1* launches for a journey that includes a soft landing on the moon.

January 27, 1967........ Astronauts Gus Grissom, Ed White, and Roger Chaffee are killed in the launchpad fire of *Apollo 1*.

April 24, 1967............. Cosmonaut Vladimir Komarov dies during the first manned launch of *Soyuz*.

July 1, 1968................ The Treaty on the Non-Proliferation of Nuclear Weapons is signed by the United States and the Soviet Union.

December 21, 1968..... The crew of *Apollo 8* become the first people to orbit the moon.

July 20, 1969.............. Americans Neil Armstrong and Buzz Aldrin become the first people to walk on the moon.

Introduction ▶
The Race to the Moon

What is the
Space Race?

The Space Race was the competition between the United States and the Soviet Union to explore space using manned and unmanned spacecraft. Superiority in space would demonstrate the superiority of the winner back on Earth.

Neil Armstrong's first steps on the lunar surface in 1969 captivated the world like no other event in human history. People everywhere stopped what they were doing to watch and listen as someone set foot on another celestial object for the very first time. It was an incredible achievement, one that would be repeated five more times.

Many people think of the first moon landing as the result of human drive, intelligence, and daring—which is certainly true. But what were the real reasons behind the decision to go to the moon? What did it take to get there? And why haven't we been back?

EARLY ROCKETS

Today's rockets are incredible feats of engineering. They are capable of generating enough power to fling space probes to the edges of the solar system and send car-sized robots to Mars.

The earliest and simplest rockets, fireworks, are still familiar to us. Around 100 CE, the Chinese began experimenting with a simple type of explosive powder, similar to gunpowder.

Eventually, gunpowder-filled bamboo tubes were attached to arrows, which helped keep them pointed in the right direction. This was the first example of a solid-fuel rocket. They were even used in war. In 1232, devices called fire-arrows were used by the Chinese in battle against the Mongols.

Most of the rockets at the time, however, were used either in firework displays or in battles to scare and frighten the enemy. It wasn't until the twentieth century that rockets grew beyond their primitive beginnings.

DREAMING OF SPACEFLIGHT

In the 1865 science fiction classic by Jules Verne (1828–1905), *From Earth to the Moon*, three adventurers are fired from a giant gun to explore the moon. Although the story was fictional, it inspired many people to explore ways of making it a reality.

In 1903, Russian school teacher and scientist Konstantin Tsiolkovsky (1857–1935) published *Exploration of Cosmic Space by Means of Reaction Devices*. Tsiolkovsky described how rockets could be used to leave the earth and circle it, just as the moon does. He used physics and mathematics to determine the speed a ship would need to escape the earth's gravitational pull, about 25,000 miles per hour.

Multi-stage rockets, airlocks to safely move between a spacecraft and the vacuum of space, and even whole cities above the earth were described in the book. Tsiolkovsky was a visionary, and his concepts would one day make their way to the moon.

THE LEGEND OF WAN HU

According to legend, a Chinese official named Wan Hu attached dozens of rockets to the back of a chair. Once lit, there was an incredible sound, and when the clouds of smoke eventually cleared, Wan Hu was nowhere to be found. Hundreds of years later, the rocket chair would make a return as a testing device! Check out this video.

🔍 Wan Hu rocket chair video

BLAST FACT

Early fireworks in China used saltpeter, sulfur, and charcoal dust to give them a bang! Occasionally, instead of exploding, they rocketed away.

In 1923, the Romanian-born Hermann Oberth (1894–1989) published *The Rocket into Planetary Space*, which outlined how a rocket could escape Earth's atmosphere and orbit the planet. Oberth realized that to do so, a new, more powerful type of rocket engine was needed.

In 1926, the American physicist Robert Goddard (1882–1945) changed rocketry forever. Goddard, inspired by the stories of Jules Verne, H.G. Wells, and other science fiction writers, was the first to develop a liquid-fueled rocket engine. This was a much more powerful way to propel a rocket through the atmosphere. With the liquid-fueled rocket engine, Goddard was able to achieve unprecedented heights with his simple rockets.

Despite his success, rocketry remained a hobby to most people. It wasn't until World War II that this type of power was recognized for its effectiveness in battle.

Robert Goddard is on the far left in this 1940 photograph.

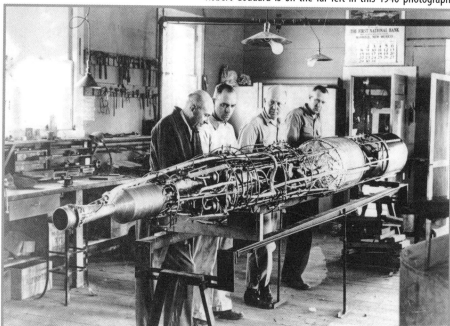

credit: National Geographic Society

THE ROCKET IN WAR

Near the end of World War II, Europe was terrorized by a new German weapon—the V-2. Standing nearly 50 feet tall and carrying about 1 ton of explosives, the German V-2 rockets were unlike anything used in war before.

Launched from German-occupied Holland, these "vengeance weapons" could reach London in just five minutes. There was no way to shoot them down. An early autopilot system onboard helped steer the missile to its target without any help from controllers on the ground.

Capable of flying 50 miles high and traveling more than 500 miles, the liquid-fueled rocket crashed to Earth at nearly twice the speed of sound. There was little anyone could do to avoid its impact.

> At the time, it was one of the most advanced and terrifying machines ever built.

The chief engineer behind the German rockets was Wernher von Braun (1912–1977), a life-long champion of space flight and exploration and a pupil of Hermann Oberth. Also inspired by the science fiction classics of H.G. Wells and Jules Verne, von Braun joined the German army during World War II to build what would become the V-2.

In 1945, as the war began to draw to an end, von Braun realized that Germany was going to lose the war. He decided it made more sense for him to surrender to the Americans than to the Soviet army. Most of his staff agreed with him. Whatever country gained von Braun and his associates gained all of their knowledge as well.

DEADLY WEAPONRY

More than 1,300 V-2s were used by Germany against England at the end of the war, killing several thousand people. However, the biggest toll of lives was in the construction of the rockets themselves. By some estimates, more than 20,000 slave laborers died building the weapons in a secret factory called Mittelwerk.

BLAST FACT

During the War of 1812, British troops used early rockets to attack Fort McHenry, prompting Francis Scott Key to write the lyrics "the rockets' red glare," which later became part of "The Star-Spangled Banner."

OPERATION PAPERCLIP

Both the United States and the Soviet Union were eager to learn about the German rockets. It was the United States that won the first stage of the Space Race with Wernher von Braun's surrender.

The Americans brought the German rocket scientists and almost all of their technology back to the United States under a program called Operation Paperclip. In the United States after the war, the German scientists continued their experiments with larger and more powerful rockets.

With the Soviet Union losing out on the advanced German technology, many Western countries assumed the Soviets didn't have the ability to build their own rockets—but they were wrong.

THE LAUNCH OF *SPUTNIK*

On October 4, 1957, history was changed forever. *Sputnik*, a tiny artificial satellite measuring only 22 inches across, was placed into orbit by the Soviet Union. The world, and especially the United States, was shocked. Suddenly, the Soviets were capable of lifting something into space. More ominously, they had a rocket that could deliver a nuclear bomb anywhere on Earth.

And with that, the Space Race began.

A replica of *Sputnik*, the first artificial satellite to be put into outer space

credit: NSSDC, NASA

In *The Space Race: How the Cold War Put Humans on the Moon*, you'll explore the history behind the Space Race and discover how the Cold War drove one of the greatest achievements of the twentieth century. You'll examine the people, places, and events that shaped the world during the drive to be the first nation to plant a flag on the moon, then see how the Space Race in turn affected events back on Earth.

You can listen to the sound *Sputnik* sent back to Earth at the NASA website.

PS

 Listen to Sputnik

KEY QUESTIONS

- **How might the Space Race have been different if German engineers had surrendered to the Russians instead of the Americans?**

- **How does science fiction inform real scientific progress? Can one exist without the other?**

Inquire & Investigate

VOCAB LAB 📖

Write down what you think each word means. What root words can you find to help you? What does the context of the word tell you?

Cold War, engineering, lunar, orbit, satellite, science fiction, Space Race, and **technology**.

Compare your definitions with those of your friends or classmates. Did you all come up with the same meanings? Turn to the text and glossary if you need help.

FIRST-PERSON ACCOUNT

The Cold War and Space Race were very important events in history. People around the world lived through the struggle between the United States and the Soviet Union, and millions tuned in to witness humanity's first steps on a different world. Do you know someone who lived through these events?

- **Interview a family member or friend who experienced the Cold War and Space Race up close.** Questions to consider include the following.

  - How was living through the Cold War different from today?

  - Did it affect their everyday life?

  - Were they ever afraid during the Cold War? Why or why not?

  - Did they watch the moon landing? How did they and their friends and family react?

  - How did it feel to watch such an important moment in human history? Did they know how special it was at the time?

> **To investigate more,** present their story however you think best represents their experience. You could write an essay, create a presentation, film a documentary—it's up to you!

Chapter 1 ▶
The Rise of Communism

How are communist
countries and
democracies
different?

In a communist country, the government controls much of the industry, economy, and even the daily lives of its citizens. In a democracy, citizens have far more freedom to choose how the country operates.

What kind of government does your country have? Today, most countries practice some form of democracy, where citizens have rights such as the right to free speech and the ability to freely elect their own leaders. But in the early twentieth century, a new form of government appeared, one that would change the course of history.

What led to that new form of government? The Industrial Revolution, which began during the 1700s in England. As people went to work manufacturing new products, large cities and factories began to replace small towns and farming.

By the mid-1800s, the Industrial Revolution had brought change to nearly every country on Earth. People from the countryside left their farms and villages to work in factories in bustling, growing cities. To take advantage of the growing demand for goods, most countries practiced an economic system called capitalism. In capitalism, individuals own businesses and factories. Owners are free to keep the money they earn.

In the nineteenth century, governments did little to control how people did business. This meant that many people worked in dangerous conditions for long hours with little pay. As a result, the wealthiest members of society kept most of the money while the laborers did most of the work. To many people, this was an unfair and immoral system.

In 1848, the German philosophers Karl Marx (1818–1883) and Friedrich Engels (1820–1895) published *The Communist Manifesto*. In it, they argued that a revolution by the working class would eventually overthrow the industrial-capitalists. There would be no money and no property—everyone would get what they needed if they worked as much as they could. This collective form of government and economics was called communism.

The idea slowly gained a following around the world.

Calling themselves Marxists, people wanted to help start the revolution Marx and Engels had described and change the world. Seventy years after *The Communist Manifesto* was published, a Marxist revolution in the Russian Empire would do just that.

THE BOLSHEVIK REVOLUTION

In the early twentieth century, the Russian Empire was the largest country in the world. Stretching from present-day Poland to the Pacific coast of Siberia, it was a diverse nation of mostly rural farmers and villagers. The unpopular Tsar Nicholas II had been in power since 1894. He often exiled or executed those who opposed him and his regime.

From 1547 to 1917, the Russian rulers were called tsars.

During World War I (1914–1918), the huge loss of Russian lives on the battlefield plus the shortages of food and fuel at home resulted in an uprising among the Russian people. Factories and farms, already hurting from the tsar's policies, shut down in protest. People took to the streets, often clashing with tsarist supports. Faced with a violent revolution, Nicholas II abdicated his throne in 1917 and stepped down as the ruler of the Russian Empire.

In the chaos that followed, a group of Marxist revolutionaries called the Bolsheviks took over the government. The revolution was led by Vladimir Lenin (1870–1924), a Marxist who'd been imprisoned by the tsar for his political beliefs. With Lenin in control, Russia quickly withdrew from World War I, leaving its European allies to fight Germany and the Central powers alone. Angered, many of Russia's former allies supported the tsarist White Army against the Bolshevik Red Army in the brutal Russian Civil War.

A NEW NATION IS BORN

When the Russian Civil War ended in 1922, the Bolshevik Red Army had won. The Bolsheviks changed their name to the Communist Party and began to transform the former Russian Empire. Communism was the goal, but the new system couldn't be put in place overnight. The old economic structure was too much a part of life, and would need to be taken apart gradually. Instead, socialism was implemented to help bridge the gap between capitalism and the communist ideal. A new nation calling itself the Union of Soviet Socialist Republics (USSR) emerged from the old Russian Empire, with Vladimir Lenin as its leader.

In the first years under Lenin, most factories and businesses were nationalized. They were seized from their owners and put under the control of the Soviet state.

If you were a factory owner, what might your reaction be?

Millions of people lost their businesses, property, and jobs. Protests were common. The Soviets often dealt with uprisings by using deadly force, punishing and even executing those who stood in the way of change. Despite his ruthless tactics, Lenin didn't compare to his successor, who became one of the most feared and brutal dictators in history.

THE MAN OF STEEL

When Vladimir Lenin died in 1924, Joseph Stalin (1878–1953) took over the leadership of the Communist Party and the Soviet Union. Stalin was aware that the capitalist nations of the West produced far more food and goods than the old Russian Empire. In response, he began a massive campaign to turn the Soviet Union into a modern industrial nation—by force.

Millions of farmers and villagers were made to work in factories and on huge collective farms, all for the good of the nation. In just 10 years, Stalin's plans transformed the Soviet Union into an industrial giant. Anyone opposed to his policies and methods was sent to labor camps or executed without a trial.

Touting his success, Stalin built a cult of personality around himself, using state-run newspapers and radio stations to praise his leadership and denounce his opponents. To keep his iron grip on the nation, he sent the secret police to round up his rivals.

WHAT IS SOCIALISM?

Today, socialism has many different meanings. In most countries, socialism is viewed as an effort to ensure that all citizens have the same opportunities regardless of social status. The method of providing those opportunities differs greatly among countries. Check out this video to learn more about the differences between capitalism, socialism, and communism.

capitalism, socialism, one minute

Without a trial, anyone suspected of the slightest resistance to Stalin and his methods was often tortured, sent to one of the labor camps known as the gulag, or executed. People were afraid to speak out for fear of vanishing. Historians estimate that more than 20 million people lost their lives under Stalin's regime.

As word of Stalin's brutal socialist system spread, some people in the United States began to be afraid. Could a communist revolution happen in America?

THE RED SCARE

After the Russian Revolution, many in the United States were suspicious of the Soviets and their socialist government. Out of fear of a communist uprising at home, a government committee was created to look into what were called un-American activities inside the United States. Fear of communism spread across the nation, with the FBI going so far as to illegally break into homes and businesses of suspected communist party members and sympathizers.

Protests and rallies sometimes turned violent. The Red Scare stirred up feelings of nationalism, and immigrants often became targets of violence. Some Russian immigrants were even deported and sent back to a country that was very different from the one they'd left.

The Soviets had their own issues of trust with the United States. The capitalist Americans had supported the tsarist forces during the Russian Civil War, a fact the Communist Party couldn't forget. But once both nations entered World War II, they found themselves uneasy allies against a common enemy intent on ending the ways of life in both nations.

LARGER THAN LIFE

A cult of personality can happen when a person or group in power uses their influence to portray themselves as heroic, perfect, and incapable of mistakes. Totalitarian regimes often use propaganda to promote their leaders and silence their opponents. As a result, followers often idolize the personality in charge. Can you think of any examples of personality cults that exist today?

WORLD WAR II

Although World War II started on September 1, 1939, with Germany's invasion of Poland, neither the United States nor the Soviet Union immediately joined the fight against Adolf Hitler (1889–1945). The United States was still reeling from World War I and the Great Depression of the 1930s. It was reluctant to get involved in another war an ocean away.

Stalin had seen the rise of Hitler and knew that Soviet forces were not ready for the coming war. In August 1939, Hitler and Stalin signed the German-Soviet Nonaggression Pact, agreeing to not attack each other. This gave Stalin time to rebuild the Soviet military and allowed Hitler to invade Poland unchallenged.

> Secretly, the two nations also agreed on how to divide Eastern Europe after the war.

Japan joined Italy and Germany a year later. Then, in June 1941, Hitler betrayed Stalin and invaded the Soviet Union. Caught off guard, the "Man of Steel" was furious. With the nonaggression pact broken, Stalin had no choice but to join Britain and France against Nazi Germany.

On December 7, 1941, the Japanese attacked the American naval base at Pearl Harbor, Hawaii. This devastating assault shocked the United States and gave President Franklin D. Roosevelt (1882–1945) no choice but to declare war on the Axis powers.

Despite the mistrust between the Western nations and the Soviets, they needed to trust each other if they were going to win. In Hitler, they faced a maniacal dictator who enslaved and slaughtered his own people and who had at his disposal the expertise to devise weapons the world had never seen before.

BLAST FACT

In a 1939 poll conducted by Roper, nearly 90 percent of Americans surveyed said that the United States should not get involved in the growing war.

THE V-2

The V-2, or "vengeance weapon," was one of Hitler's last efforts to turn around the Allied advance on the German capital of Berlin. By the end of the war, more than 1,300 of these ballistic missiles were fired at England and hundreds more at France and Belgium, killing nearly 3,000 people.

On September 8, 1944, a new kind of weapon appeared in battle. Unlike the German bombers, it outran its own roar and struck without warning. It fell on quiet neighborhoods and busy city streets alike, reducing homes and businesses to piles of rubble. There was no way to defend against the new weapon—it terrorized all of those who lived within its range.

The V-2 was the world's first ballistic missile. Standing 46 feet tall and carrying a 2,200-pound explosive warhead, the missile's powerful, liquid-fueled rocket motor took the rocket to heights of 50 miles. It could hit targets hundreds of miles away. At its top speed of 3,500 miles per hour, it was twice as fast as a bullet and could reach its target in less than five minutes. It was an incredible feat of engineering. Its creator, Wernher von Braun, had dreams of using his rocket as something other than a weapon.[1]

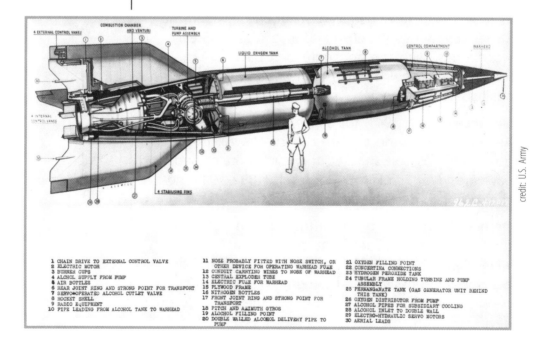

credit: U.S. Army

1 CHAIN DRIVE TO EXTERNAL CONTROL VALVE
2 ELECTRIC MOTOR
3 BURNER CUPS
4 ALCOHOL SUPPLY FROM PUMP
5 AIR BOTTLES
6 REAR JOINT RING AND STRONG POINT FOR TRANSPORT
7 SERVO-OPERATED ALCOHOL OUTLET VALVE
8 ROCKET SHELL
9 RADIO EQUIPMENT
10 PIPE LEADING FROM ALCOHOL TANK TO WARHEAD

11 NOSE PROBABLY FITTED WITH NOSE SWITCH, OR OTHER DEVICE FOR OPERATING WARHEAD FUZE
12 CONDUIT CARRYING WIRES TO NOSE OF WARHEAD
13 CENTRAL EXPLODER TUBE
14 ELECTRIC FUZE FOR WARHEAD
15 PLYWOOD FRAME
16 NITROGEN BOTTLES
17 FRONT JOINT RING AND STRONG POINT FOR TRANSPORT
18 PITCH AND AZIMUTH GYROS
19 ALCOHOL FILLING POINT
20 DOUBLE WALLED ALCOHOL DELIVERY PIPE TO PUMP

21 OXYGEN FILLING POINT
22 CONCERTINA CONNECTIONS
23 HYDROGEN PEROXIDE TANK
24 TUBULAR FRAME HOLDING TURBINE AND PUMP ASSEMBLY
25 PERMANGANATE TANK (GAS GENERATOR UNIT BEHIND THIS TANK)
26 OXYGEN DISTRIBUTOR FROM PUMP
27 ALCOHOL PIPES FOR SUBSIDIARY COOLING
28 ALCOHOL INLET TO DOUBLE WALL
29 ELECTRO-HYDRAULIC SERVO MOTORS
30 AERIAL LEADS

As a child growing up in Germany, Wernher von Braun loved science fiction. He read books by Jules Verne and H.G. Wells and was fascinated by the idea of exploring space. After studying Hermann Oberth's *The Rocket into Planetary Space*, he was convinced rockets were the key to exploring space.

He joined the German Society for Space Travel, a local rocket club where he could put his skills to use alongside other rocket enthusiasts while he studied math and physics. In the early 1930s, the German military took notice of the club's work and von Braun was soon using their resources to build powerful rockets.

While he worked on rockets, von Braun joined the Nazi party and later became a member of the SS, the feared paramilitary organization that committed some of the worst atrocities of the war. Although he wasn't interested in politics, von Braun believed his career depended on his obedience to the regime. However, he kept his dream of exploration, telling several people that he'd only ever wanted to use his rockets to explore space. For his comments, he was arrested for treason. But Hitler was desperate for any advantage, and von Braun was released to finish work on his revolutionary weapon.

> By the time the V-2 was ready, the war in Europe was nearly over.

As the Allies approached the German capital of Berlin at the end of the war, they were eager to capture any German rocket technology they could find—including the engineers and scientists behind it. Knowing the war was lost, von Braun assembled his team. Europe was in ruins, and the brutal Soviet army was getting close. If the team wanted to follow its dreams of spaceflight, there was only one choice—surrender to the Americans.

BLAST FACT

Von Braun wanted to explore space, but Hitler's rise to power meant that von Braun had to build a weapon, not a spaceship.

SLAVE LABOR

To build the V-2, the Nazi regime forced thousands of prisoners from the Buchenwald and Dora concentration camps to work in an underground facility called Mittelwerk. Under terrible conditions, an estimated 20,000 people died while constructing the V-2. That's far more than were killed by its use. Von Braun claimed to have no knowledge of the use of slave labor, although historians now doubt his claims.

After Germany's defeat in May 1945, von Braun and his group of rocket scientists found themselves swept up in Operation Paperclip, a secret effort to bring German engineers and scientists to the United States. Rocket parts and plans were quickly and quietly packed and sent to New Mexico, followed by their German designers. They would now be building missiles for the U.S. military.

Although the Americans took most of the rockets and engineers, the Soviets recovered some V-2s with the help of a small group of German defectors. Despite their knowledge, the German rocket scientists were not von Braun. Without him, Stalin needed to look among his own people to find someone to lead the Soviet missile program.

However, the man with the knowledge and experience to tackle the problem was in prison.

SERGEI KOROLEV

The lives of the German rocket engineer Wernher von Braun and his Russian counterpart, Sergei Korolev (1906–1966), began in similar ways. Like von Braun, Korolev was interested in rockets at a young age. Both were influenced by the work of Konstantin Tsiolkovsky, the Russian physicist and teacher who wrote about the potential of rockets to explore the solar system.

During the 1930s, Korolev's experiments with rocket engines caught the attention of the Soviet military. With support from the army, he studied how rockets could be used to carry weapons or even people.

NUCLEAR WAR

The use of nuclear weapons by the United States remains one of the most controversial moments in history. Some argue that the use of nuclear weapons ultimately saved lives, while others believe that such destructive power should never have been used at all. You can learn more about the aftermath of the atomic bombs here.

U.S. history Manhattan Project

In 1938, his work was interrupted by the "Great Terror," a period of state-sponsored executions and imprisonment of some people in the Communist Party. Along with millions of others, Korolev was tortured and sent to Siberia as a prisoner in the Soviet gulag.

At the end of the war, it was clear to the Soviet experts examining the German rockets that someone was needed to decipher the complex V-2, and that someone needed a history of rocketry. Suddenly, Korolev was released from his prison sentence and given the task of learning everything he could from the V-2 in order to build a more powerful rocket for the Soviet Union.

Atomic cloud over Hiroshima, taken from *Enola Gay*, the bomber from which the first atomic bomb was dropped

credit: 509th Operations Group

THE ATOMIC AGE

The war in Europe was over, but the fight against Japan continued. On August 6, 1945, the United States dropped an atomic bomb on the city of Hiroshima, Japan. The effects were devastating, consuming the city in a massive fireball underneath a mushroom-shaped cloud.

An estimated 70,000 people were incinerated instantly. At least 100,000 would die over time from cancer and other effects of radiation exposure. Three days later, another bomb was dropped on the city of Nagasaki, Japan, with similar deadly results. In less than a week, Japan surrendered, ending the most destructive war in human history.[2]

With the annihilation of Hiroshima and Nagasaki, the world had entered the atomic age. Nations were awed by the power and violence of the atomic weapons and feared the devastating effects of their use.

> With atomic weapons, the United States was now the most powerful nation on Earth, capable of erasing entire cities in a flash of light.

As the war was coming to its conclusion, Stalin saw the United States and the Soviet Union as equals, separated by ideologies and oceans. But nuclear weapons suddenly tipped the balance to the Americans. Without a nuclear weapon of its own, the Soviet Union was at a disadvantage.

Stalin was determined that it wouldn't stay that way for long.

KEY QUESTIONS

- How did the Russian Revolution lead to the state of communism in the Soviet Union?

- Was it morally right for the Americans to drop the atomic bombs on Japan at the end of the Second World War?

COMMUNISM, SOCIALISM, AND CAPITALISM TODAY

Capitalism, socialism, and communism have different meanings for different countries. While the Soviet Union no longer exists, there are other nations that practice different kinds of socialism, and a few that still seek to reach the communist ideal. Many more nations practice capitalism and socialism together.

- **Research a communist nation, a socialist nation, and a nation that practices capitalism.**

  - How does each country define its economic and social systems?

  - Do they consider themselves more of one than the others?

- **Have any of the nations you chose changed from one type of social or economic system to another?** If so, what was the result? And if not, why?

- **What are the benefits and challenges each of the counties faces?** How do these countries compare?

> **To investigate more,** research a nation that was considered part of the former Soviet Union. What is it like today? What form of government, social, and economic system does it use? How does it compare to the country you live in?

BACKGROUND CHECKS

Wernher von Braun was considered a hero for his work on the space program. However, after his death in 1977, his participation in wartime atrocities as a member of the Nazi Party came under closer scrutiny.

When von Braun was first interviewed after World War II, he claimed he'd not participated in the decision to use slave laborers from concentration camps to produce the V-2.

- **Research his life.** What do you think? Is there evidence that von Braun was not truthful about his work during the war?

- **Many people claimed that von Braun and his associates were excluded from prosecution in exchange for their knowledge of rocketry.** What do you think were the considerations behind the U.S. government's decision to bring the German scientists to America during Operation Paperclip?

- **Should America's victory in the Space Race be viewed differently considering von Braun's history?**

> **To investigate more,** consider that Wernher von Braun wasn't the only foreign scientist to come to the United States. Research other scientists who have made the United States their home. Why did they choose to come to this country? What were their contributions to science? Did they have questionable backgrounds like von Braun?

Chapter 2 ▶
The Cold War Begins

THE COLD WAR BETWEEN THE COMMUNIST SOVIET UNION AND THE CAPITALIST UNITED STATES LAID THE FOUNDATION FOR THE SPACE RACE.

How did the start of the Cold War spur the Space Race?

AFTER WORLD WAR II, RUSSIA SET UP COMMUNIST REGIMES IN EASTERN EUROPE TO STAND AGAINST THE DEMOCRATIC, CAPITALIST COUNTRIES IN WESTERN EUROPE.

BERLIN WAS SPLIT BETWEEN EAST AND WEST INTO DEMOCRATIC AND SOCIALIST HALVES, THE BEGINNING OF THE "IRON CURTAIN" THAT FELL OVER EASTERN EUROPE.

ALMOST A DECADE AFTER THE START OF THE COLD WAR, RUSSIA WON THE FIRST LEG IN THE SPACE RACE WITH THE LAUNCH OF SPUTNIK IN 1957.

As the United States and the Soviet Union began to experience tension on the ground, they also began to compete to be first in space.

As World War II, the deadliest war in history, came to an end, a new world took shape. The United States and Soviet Union were now the two most powerful nations on Earth, and both countries raced to assert themselves while the threat of a different kind of war loomed.

After the surrender of Germany and Japan, distrust between the United States and Soviet Union grew quickly. Despite objections by their former allies, the Soviets installed communist governments across Eastern Europe. These puppet regimes gave Stalin partners in the competition against the American-friendly democracies of Western Europe.

By the summer of 1948, the wartime alliance between the West and the Soviets was all but over. The formation of West Germany and its capital of Bonn infuriated the Soviets. In response, Stalin declared a blockade of the West German city of West Berlin, which had been partitioned from East Berlin at the end of World War II.

The Soviets shut off all road and rail access to the city. To avoid starvation in West Berlin, the United States and Great Britain launched a massive effort to deliver food and supplies the only way they could— by airplane.

For 318 days, day and night, the Berlin Airlift delivered millions of tons of food, fuel, and supplies to the defiant city. More than 270,000 flights landed. It was an embarrassing political disaster for the Soviet Union, with most of the world siding against Stalin and his attempt to capture West Berlin by starvation.[1]

Unwilling to start a war while his country was being rebuilt, Stalin ended the Berlin blockade on May 12, 1949. The West had won because the Soviets were outmatched by America's military and technological abilities. Stalin was desperate to even the odds and prove that there was more than one nation capable of leading the world.

A cargo plane lands in West Berlin, 1948

credit: U.S. Air Force

The separation of East and West Berlin

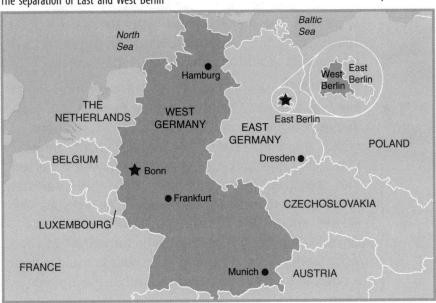

Just months after the end of the blockade, the Soviets shocked the world by detonating their first nuclear weapon. America, surprised by the incredible progress of what many had considered a backward nation, announced its intention to develop more powerful nuclear weapons. The Soviets did the same.

As the 1940s ended, two nations with very different ideas of economics, government, and world affairs now had the most powerful weapon on Earth. The nuclear arms race had begun, and the perfect delivery method for nuclear weapons was already being tested.

THE ICBM

Now that both nuclear powers had the bomb, they wanted the intercontinental ballistic missile (ICBM), a rocket capable of delivering a nuclear warhead anywhere on Earth. At the U.S. Army Ordinance Proving Ground in White Sands, New Mexico, von Braun again found himself working in a country more interested in weapons than spaceflight.

Test launches of the captured V-2 rockets were successful. The rockets could fly as far as the edge of space. Von Braun, looking toward the future, hoped the rockets would eventually carry passengers.

In the USSR, Sergei Korolev was in a position much like von Braun's. After successfully flying a V-2, the Soviet military wanted its own ICBM to compete with the United States. Korolev had already begun plans for huge rockets capable of carrying a person into space, but the Soviet army was more interested in weapons than space exploration. As a result, Korolev made sure that his powerful missile was capable of putting something—or someone—in space, while persuading those in charge that it could deliver a nuclear warhead to anywhere within the United States.

Testing a captured V-2 in White Sands, New Mexico

credit: U.S. Air Force

As the nuclear adversaries worked on their missile programs, the world settled into the new realities of a Cold War that everyone hoped would not turn hot. Confrontation between the nations continued. The outbreak of the Korean War in 1950 pitted the American-backed, democratic South Korea against the Soviet-backed, communist North Korea.

Some military commanders wanted to authorize the use of nuclear weapons, but the decision was never made. Although the United States and the USSR never fought each other directly, the Korean war was a struggle between the two nations that foreshadowed the direction the Cold War would take.

Despite a booming economy and the birth of rock-and-roll music, the 1950s in America were marked with paranoia and suspicion. Several Soviet spies were arrested early in the decade for stealing nuclear secrets. These arrests made people fear that communism was not just an outside threat.

U.S. Senator Joseph McCarthy (1908–1957) led hearings that accused members of the military and government of being secret communists, intent on destroying America from the inside. The House Un-American Activities Committee (HUAC) investigated Hollywood actors, writers, and producers for suspected communist connections. Despite their innocence, many of the accused were blacklisted and unable to work in entertainment.

News of interesting experiments in the New Mexico desert provided some relief from the seemingly daily warnings about communism and nuclear war that marked the 1950s. The rockets from World War II were becoming more powerful, reaching greater heights, and flying longer distances as they explored the edge of space. Wernher von Braun saw the public's growing interest in rocketry and spaceflight as an opportunity.

POPULARIZING SPACE

In 1950, von Braun and his team were moved to the U.S. Army Redstone Arsenal near Huntsville, Alabama, to continue work on ballistic missiles. While there, he wrote articles for American magazines describing his vision of the future. It included spinning outposts in space, bases on the moon and Mars, and even space tourism. How could anyone resist?

People fell in love with von Braun's visions of peaceful space exploration. It was a welcome break from the threat of nuclear war.

In the Soviet Union, however, there were no television shows or magazine covers for Sergei Korolev. Although he followed von Braun's progress closely, Korolev's very existence was kept secret, even from government and military officials.

> In secret circles, Sergei Korolev was known only as the "Chief Designer."

Despite his anonymity, he was as much an advocate for using rockets to explore space as von Braun, but the policy of absolute secrecy kept him from appealing to the citizens of the Soviet Union and the world. Korolev felt that von Braun was working on a space program, while he was stuck working on a missile program. To convince Moscow that a space program was worth the effort, he'd need help from both inside and outside the Soviet Union.

ANIMALS IN SPACE

As the Cold War powers struggled over their roles in the post-war world, both rocket programs moved forward as interest in spaceflight grew around the world. Von Braun's visions of cities in space seemed like science fiction, though he was confident they would become reality. But there were many questions. What kind of effect would spaceflight have on a living person? What was space really like? For people to find answers, living things needed to go into space.

On June 14, 1949, the Americans sent the rhesus monkey Albert II into space. Albert II became the first primate to cross the Kármán line, the 60-mile altitude boundary considered to be the beginning of space. Unfortunately, Albert II did not survive the landing. However, his flight gave scientists hope that a human passenger could survive a trip to space.

ANIMALS IN SPACE

Unfortunately, both Albert II and his predecessor, Albert I, did not survive their flights. Their deaths made it clear that there was much to learn before a person could safely ride a rocket. In 1959, the monkeys Baker and Able became the first American mammals to fly to space and arrive back on Earth safe and sound. You can read about their journey in a news article and watch a video of their experience at these websites.

 space monkeys news

 Baker Able video

As the United States launched several more monkeys into space, the Soviets conducted their own experiments with canine passengers. On July 22, 1951, Dezik and Tsygan became the first dogs in space, flying a suborbital path similar to Albert II's that brought them safely back to Earth.

Both nations learned a lot about the environment of space and its effect on living creatures, giving hope to von Braun and Korolev that their dreams of exploring the solar system might become reality.

In early 1953, President Dwight D. Eisenhower (1890–1969) was sworn in as president of the United States. A former Army general who commanded American forces in World War II, Eisenhower was seen by Americans as the person needed to stand up to communism and Joseph Stalin.

A few months later, however, after the death of Joseph Stalin in 1953, the Soviet Union had its own new leader.

Nikita Khrushchev (1894–1971), the new Communist Party leader, condemned the Man of Steel's purges and the personality cult that he'd built around himself and his followers. Khrushchev's blunt criticism of his predecessor shocked the Communist Party and the world.

Both von Braun and Korolev hoped the new world leaders would take up the cause of space exploration. Despite von Braun's appeal to the public, there was still little funding for missiles beyond their intended military use. It would take an international effort to focus both governments on exploring space.

The 1953 death of Joseph Stalin was a relief to many in the Soviet Union and around the world. His great purge killed millions of his own citizens, with millions more exiled to the gulag. Both the world and many within the Soviet Union were glad to see the terrible dictator gone.

THE BEGINNING OF
THE SPACE RACE

In 1955, President Eisenhower announced that the United States would participate in the upcoming International Geophysical Year in 1957–1958 by launching the world's first manmade satellite into orbit around Earth. It would be a peaceful demonstration of American's advanced rocketry and would show that the technology could be used for something other than war.

Von Braun was ecstatic. After years of little funding, space exploration was finally being taken seriously in the United States. His newest missile, called Redstone, could certainly put a small satellite in orbit for the International Geophysical Year.

In the Soviet Union, Korolev used the news of the Americans' intentions to convince the leadership in Moscow that a space program was necessary if the Soviets wanted to keep pace with the Americans. He argued that beating the Americans into space would be a huge victory for the country.

Not to be outdone, Nikita Khrushchev announced that the Soviet Union would also launch a satellite for the International Geophysical Year. Fortunately, Korolev's most recent design, the R-7 missile, could do just that. The first leg of the Space Race was set, with von Braun and Korolev ready to take their marks.

However, despite successful launches of the Redstone, von Braun's dream was put on hold in favor of the U.S. Navy's Project Vanguard. Based on a sounding rocket, Vanguard was not designed to carry a warhead and was only for scientific use.

BLAST FACT

Intended as a worldwide effort to study many branches of earth science, the International Geophysical Year drew researchers from 67 countries eager to cooperate.

Von Braun pleaded with the government to reconsider. Project Vanguard had serious problems, he argued, and was far behind schedule. He warned that if Vanguard faced any more trouble, the United States would miss its chance to put the first artificial satellite in orbit.

Von Braun was unable to change the minds of the government officials in charge. Unfortunately for the United States, von Braun proved to be right.

A SOVIET MOON

On October 4, 1957, Korolev's R-7 left the launch pad on a pillar of flame. Unlike all the other rocket flights before it, this one did not return to Earth. When it reached its designated speed and altitude, it released into space a small, silver sphere just 22 inches across. As this sphere circled the globe, it broadcast a simple radio signal that could be heard around the world.

> This was *Sputnik*, the world's first artificial satellite and the first man-made object to orbit the Earth.

The launch of *Sputnik* caught the Americans off-guard. For the second time, the Soviet Union surprised the West with its engineering and scientific capabilities.

Headlines around the world declared the stunning achievement a historic moment for humanity and a triumph for the Soviets. To the public eye, the balance of power between the two nations had tipped in favor of the Soviet Union. If they could put a satellite in space, they could put a nuclear bomb anywhere in the world.

A model of *Sputnik*, the first artificial satellite

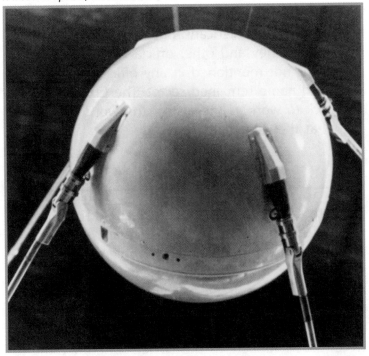

With *Sputnik* flying overhead, all kinds of possibilities emerged. Could the Soviets spy on the United States from above, far out of reach of airplanes or missiles? Could they use it to drop an atomic bomb?

On November 3, 1957, the Soviets did the seemingly impossible again. *Sputnik 2* carried a small dog named Laika into orbit. This was an even greater accomplishment than the satellite the Soviets had lofted up just a month before. Not only could they put satellites into space, they also had the capability to keep an animal alive for at least a short time as it circled the earth.

Newspapers around the world speculated that it was just a matter of time before a person would ride into space on top of a Soviet rocket.

SPECIAL REPORT

When *Sputnik* was launched, it caused a sensation around the world. You can watch a CBS news clip from October 6, 1957, at this website. How do you think people reacted to hearing about *Sputnik*? Why do you think people were worried that the satellite was emitting a code?

🔍 CBS Sputnik news

Korolev was ecstatic about the successful flights. He'd achieved his lifelong goal of reaching orbit, and he'd beaten the Americans. But while congratulations from Khrushchev and other officials poured in, his name was not mentioned in any official press. His work and name remained secret. The Chief Designer got back to work as the rest of the world waited to see what the Americans would do.

KAPUTNIK!

Eager to calm the public's fear, President Eisenhower pressured the Navy to launch Vanguard as quickly as possible. Despite continuing problems, Vanguard was prepared for launch. On December 6, the nation tuned in by radio, television, and in person to witness America's first shot at a satellite. It was time for the Americans to show the world that they were just as capable as the Soviets when it came to missiles and rockets.

When the countdown reached zero, the Vanguard rocket rose slowly a few inches from its launch pad and exploded in a massive fireball. Headlines such as "Kaputnik!" and "Flopnik!" ridiculed the disastrous attempt. It was a huge public embarrassment for President Eisenhower and for the nation as a whole.

Just how far behind was the United States? In the wake of the Vanguard failure, von Braun's Redstone rocket became America's best chance to put a satellite into space.

After several weeks of hurried preparation and tests, von Braun and his team had their rocket on the launch pad. With the nation tuned in to watch on January 31, 1958, a Redstone rocket successfully carried *Explorer 1* into the history books as the United States' first artificial satellite.

For the Americans, *Explorer 1* was a small victory, but for von Braun, it was a personal triumph.

Launch of *Explorer 1*

credit: NASA

While the Soviets kept the identity of the Chief Designer and the details of his R-7 rocket a secret, the world now knew that the Soviets had a very powerful missile. It could easily reach the United States and perhaps put a person into orbit.

The Space Race had begun.

KEY QUESTIONS

- **Why was it important to President Eisenhower and others that the space program be started on a rocket that wasn't meant to be a weapon?**

- **Are there any moral arguments about sending animals into space?**

VOCAB LAB 📖

Write down what you think each word means. What root words can you find to help you? What does the context of the word tell you?

adversary, **altitude**, **blacklist**, **paranoia**, **primate**, **satellite**, *Sputnik*, and **suborbital**.

Compare your definitions with those of your friends or classmates. Did you all come up with the same meanings? Turn to the text and glossary if you need help.

PROPAGANDA!

Stalin and the Communist Party were experts at using different forms of propaganda. Newspapers, radio, and eventually television were all used to promote the progress and exceptionalism of the Soviet State and celebrate its accomplishments while ignoring criticism and failures. Even the fine arts were subjected to censorship to ensure that a positive vision of the Soviet State was portrayed. If people failed to sufficiently praise the Communist Party or its leader, they could end up in prison—or worse.

Check out these examples of Soviet propaganda.

PS

🔎 PBS propaganda poster Soviet

🔎 animated Soviet propaganda

* **Research Soviet propaganda in any form you choose—audio, video, print, or other.**

  * How does it compare to the world today?

  * Can you think of examples of propaganda in your own country?

  * Is propaganda harmful or helpful? Try arguing each side, or debate with a classmate, family member, or friend.

> To investigate more, create your own Soviet propaganda. Make a poster, an audio recording, or video promoting the Soviet space program. Research examples and be creative!

Chapter 3 ▶
Man in Space

SINCE IT WAS A RACE, WHAT WAS THE FINISH LINE?

How did secrecy play a part in the Space Race?

The USSR kept everything about its programs secret from both the international community and its own people, while the United States shared every success and failure.

The launch of *Sputnik* by the Soviet Union was more than a turning point in the race to space. It was a huge turning point in the Cold War, too. The United States had viewed the Soviet Union as incapable of orbiting a satellite, but when *Sputnik* passed overhead, the country was reminded how wrong it was.

Khrushchev, pleased with the international recognition *Sputnik* had attracted, boasted of stockpiles of nuclear-armed ICBMs ready to launch at a moment's notice. Unable to verify the Soviet leader's claim, President Eisenhower had to take Khrushchev at his word.

The U.S. Air Force had a more powerful rocket in the Atlas missile, but the Americans didn't have a huge arsenal of them—yet. Faced with a "missile gap," the U.S. government decided it needed more missiles to ward off the Soviet threat. It was a chilling thought for the country and the world.

President Eisenhower wanted to keep American space exploration separate from the military as much as possible. To catch up to the Soviets, however, it was time to combine efforts into a single program. To do this, most programs from the Army, Navy, and Air Force were combined into a civilian agency that was responsible for the peaceful exploration of space. Some military programs still operated outside this one organization.

Von Braun, who had put the country into orbit, would join the program, but not as its head. Instead, he would work on the giant rocket of his dreams, a rocket that could take people to the moon.

THE BEGINNING OF NASA

On October 1, 1958, the National Aeronautics and Space Administration (NASA) opened its doors to take on the challenges of space flight. Just weeks after its birth, NASA made headlines when it announced the man-in-space program. Its goals were to put a person in orbit, study how space flight affects people's minds and bodies, and bring them safely back to Earth. Everyone knew the unstated hope—to be first.

> With the creation of NASA, the United States committed fully to the Space Race.

But before its goals could be accomplished, NASA had to answer a lot of questions. Could humans function in space? Could they breathe, eat, and sleep there? Could they even go to the bathroom normally? Would they go crazy being so far from home? Could a rocket be made reliable enough to safely send people on such a risky trip? What kind of spacecraft could bring them back? And who would even consider such a dangerous job?

STEM STUDY

Did the United States simply have less brain power? In 1958, Congress passed the National Defense Education Act, providing extra funding for math and science education to "catch up" to the Soviets. This act provided money for schools to focus on science, technology, engineering, and math (now called STEM), as well as college scholarships and loans for students studying these subjects. Do you study STEM subjects more than language arts and history?

THE MERCURY SEVEN

In January 1959, a quiet call went out for pilots with some very specific requirements. They needed to have college degrees, be no taller than 5 feet, 11 inches, be no heavier than 180 pounds, and have extensive experience flying the newest high-performance fighter jets.

The recruits were subjected to every kind of medical test imaginable, plus some that weren't. Blood tests were taken, and heart rate and lung capacity were measured. The men were spun in a giant centrifuge to simulate the strong g-forces they would experience during launch. Long periods of isolation, sleep deprivation, and sudden noise were used to test their ability to mentally withstand the hazards of flying in space.

The Mercury Seven

Credit: NASA/Langley Research Center

Despite the Soviet Union's lead in the Space Race, all the astronauts expressed confidence in the NASA program and were eager to be the first person in space.

On April 9, 1959, the Mercury Seven were introduced to the world. The seven future astronauts—Scott Carpenter, Gordon Cooper, John Glenn, Gus Grissom, Wally Schirra, Alan Shepard, and Deke Slayton—became instant celebrities. But, they still needed a spacecraft.

THE MERCURY CAPSULE

Early rocket experiments showed that space was a very dangerous place for humans. Scientists discovered that above Earth's atmosphere, astronauts needed protection from the vacuum of space. Without protection, bubbles would quickly form in their blood, causing it to boil.

In space, temperatures could be as high as 500 degrees Fahrenheit (250 degrees Celsius) in sunlight and as low as -150 degrees Fahrenheit (-101 degrees Celsius) in the shade.

The craft also had to be strong enough to withstand the intense forces of the launch and the estimated 3,000-degree Fahrenheit (1,649-degree Celsius) heat of reentry, all while being as light as possible. And it needed to work perfectly, every time. The task of designing such a spacecraft fell to aeronautical engineer Max Faget (1921–2004).

Faget's design for the first American spacecraft looked nothing like the spaceships of science fiction. It was small, measuring just 6 feet, 10 inches tall and 6 feet, 2½ inches at its widest. Shaped like a bell, the miniscule capsule had just enough room for one person. And it had just enough equipment to keep that person alive.

USER-FRIENDLY

During their first viewing of the capsule, the Mercury astronauts were not impressed with their new ride. There were only small portholes, and no system for manual control. Everything would be automated and controlled from the ground. The pilots argued strongly for a backup manual control system and a better view—and they won.

Small retro-rockets would slow the capsule's speed, and its blunt end was covered by a heat shield to protect it against the high temperatures of reentry. Parachutes would guide the craft to an ocean landing, where ships would pluck the capsule and astronaut from the water.

It was an ingenious design, but it wasn't the only spacecraft being readied for human flight. While the American effort was front-page news around the world, the Soviets were secretly working on their own craft and the men who would fly in it.

A diagram of the first Mercury capsule from 1959

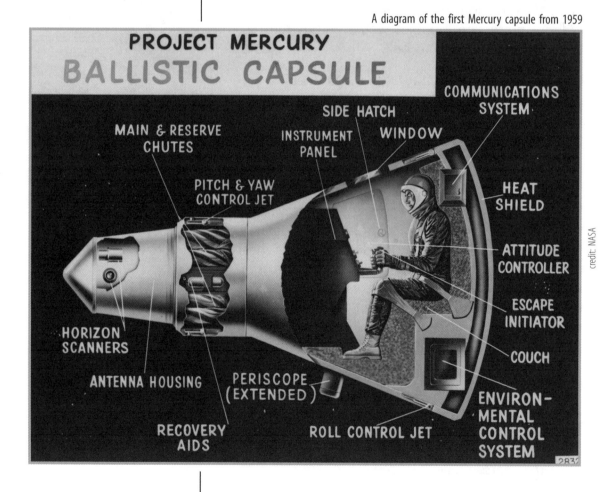

credit: NASA

THE COSMONAUTS

While the selection of the Mercury Seven drew worldwide attention, the Soviet's search for their first cosmonauts was held in secrecy, even from the candidates themselves. The Soviet search included hundreds of highly skilled pilots, who were kept in the dark about the true mission. At first, the candidates were told only that they would be evaluated for a "special flight," but the extensive testing of their mental and physical abilities led them to guess what they were being prepared for.

Eventually, 20 of the most qualified individuals were chosen.

Like their American competitors, each hoped he would be the one to beat all the others and become the first person in space. But none of them were sure how they'd get there. And who was in charge? While von Braun was a part of NASA and a household name in the United States, Korolev's identity was kept secret, even from the chosen pilots.

Until their first meeting, the cosmonauts knew Korolev only as the Chief Designer, a man with a reputation for taking big risks that almost always seemed to pay off. It was Korolev who gave them their first view of the vehicle engineered to take them to space.

A CLUB FOR MEN

In the very early days of spaceflight, both countries turned to test pilots with experience flying military aircraft. In the United States, women were not allowed to fly fighter jets or any aircraft in combat roles. As a result, they were excluded from the Mercury Program.

VOSTOK

Like the Mercury capsule, the Soviet spacecraft looked nothing like the jets the pilots were used to. There were no wings and no engines. But Vostok was also very different from the bell-shaped Mercury.

Vostok had two main parts: an instrumentation module and a spherical descent capsule. The instrumentation module contained communication equipment, experiments, and retro-rockets to slow the craft and return it to Earth. The descent capsule was the cosmonaut's cockpit, complete with an ejection seat. Instead of landing, the cosmonaut would be automatically flung from the capsule and land on his own by parachute.

Although smaller than a fighter jet, the Vostok was much larger than the Americans' spaceship, weighing 10,430 pounds compared to the Mercury's 3,000. The difference in size was due to the rockets each country would use to send them into space. Korolev's R-7 was a much more powerful machine than the Atlas D rocket used for Project Mercury, and could carry much more mass into orbit.

Both the capsules and rockets were impressive pieces of engineering. But both needed to be carefully tested before anyone climbed aboard.

FAILURE

The first test launch of the Vostok spacecraft in May 1960 began well, with the R-7 rocket performing perfectly and placing the unmanned capsule into orbit. But at the end of the mission, the retro-rockets did not burn long enough to slow the capsule for reentry. The tiny sphere skipped off the atmosphere like a stone across a pond, out of fuel and stuck in orbit. If a cosmonaut had been aboard, he would have died when the oxygen ran out.

Fortunately, the next test of the Vostok craft went much better, carrying the dogs Belka and Strelka into orbit and back home safely. The Soviets were now confident Vostok was ready for its intended passenger.

Three months after the dogs' flight, an unmanned Mercury-Redstone rocket stood ready on a launch pad at Cape Canaveral, Florida. After several delays, NASA and von Braun were desperate for a successful flight.

Politicians, military leaders, and members of the press gathered to watch. As the countdown clock reached zero, the rocket immediately roared to life— and just as quickly went quiet. Suddenly, the escape tower shot free from the capsule, careening through the sky. Onlookers ran for cover as it crashed on a nearby beach. Moments later, the parachutes popped out from the top of the Mercury capsule, covering the motionless rocket.

While both countries celebrated their successes, only the United States made its failures public. It was an embarrassing failure, but it was soon overshadowed by a more dangerous incident that followed.

An Air Force U-2 Dragon Lady

credit: U.S. Air Force

Check out the three-part press conference that introduced the Mercury Seven to the world here.

 NASA press conference 1959, part 1

 NASA press conference 1959, part 2

 NASA press conference 1959, part 3

That same summer of 1960, American pilot Gary Powers's U-2 spy plane was shot down while on a spy mission over the USSR. The American government denied it was a surveillance plane, but the capture of the pilot and the plane's wreckage made its mission obvious. Furious, Khrushchev canceled a planned summit with President Eisenhower, calling the American president untrustworthy.

It was a diplomatic embarrassment for the United States.

With the rocket failure and the capture of an American pilot, many Americans hoped that the presidential election of 1960 would help the country take the lead in the Space Race and regain its standing with the rest of the world. The new, young U.S. President John F. Kennedy (1917–1963) seemed to be just what the country needed—a fresh start.

WHO WOULD BE FIRST?

The public wanted to know who would be the first to sit atop a Mercury-Redstone rocket. If the choice was left to the people, they'd have picked John Glenn (1921–2016). The clean-cut, all-American figure was by far the most popular and well-known of the group.

Within the Mercury Seven, however, Glenn was not the most popular. His squeaky-clean image and occasional clashes with the others meant that while he was respected for his work, he was not their choice to make history. When NASA asked the Mercury Seven who should be first, they suggested Alan Shepard (1923–1998).

Born in the small town of East Derry, New Hampshire, in 1923, Shepard was interested in flight at a young age and considered the aviator Charles Lindbergh a hero. While excelling at math and science in high school, he also took jobs working on, in, and around airplanes. After serving in the Navy during WWII, Shepard graduated from flight school and became one of the youngest test pilots ever.

Intelligent and level-headed, he was respected by every member of the Mercury Program. The selection of Alan Shepard even made news in the Soviet Union, but, as with most things, it kept its choice for the first cosmonaut secret. Now the world knew who the Americans would send into space—would he beat whomever the Soviets selected?

YURI GAGARIN

Yuri Gagarin's (1934–1968) upbringing was very different from Shepard's. Gagarin was born in Klushino, Smolensk, and his family was extremely poor. Their village had no water and no electricity. The future cosmonaut was not even able to attend school, and instead learned to read and write at home. His family suffered greatly during the German invasion of World War II—they had to live in a pit while enemy soldiers took their home.

After the war, Gagarin attended makeshift classes and was considered a bright student. He went on to study farming machinery at a technical college. It was at an airfield near his school that Gagarin got his first real taste for flying, and soon he joined the military to become a fighter pilot.

For the American astronauts and Soviet cosmonauts, training for the first space flight reached a new level of intensity in 1961. While the cosmonauts worked in absolute secrecy, every move the Americans made was big news.

When officials began asking for volunteers to join a secret project, he was quickly selected, but he was forced to keep this secret even from his family. Once selected as the best pilot by the State Commission, Gagarin was ready, confident that he and the Vostok spacecraft would make history.

POYEKHALI! ("LET'S GO!")

After the embarrassing failure to leave the launch pad, NASA quickly rebounded with several Mercury-Redstone tests, including the suborbital flight of a chimpanzee named Ham. To astronaut Alan Shepard, Ham's flight proved that the rocket and capsule were safe. But several at NASA, including von Braun, decided that one more test was needed. Shepard's March 24 flight was changed to an unmanned flight, and he was scheduled instead for late April.

> Shepard was furious. He thought the extra test would cost the United States the chance to beat the Soviets.

All he could do was watch the final successful test and wait. Everyone was wondering just how close the Soviets were to their shared goal.

At 9:07 a.m. on April 12, 1961, an R-7 rocket roared to life and left the Kazakhstan steppe. The booster worked perfectly, accelerating its Vostok capsule to 17,400 miles per hour and an altitude of 203 miles. Inside, the world's first cosmonaut, Yuri Gagarin, looked through the small portholes at Earth below. He'd come a long way.

OCCUPATION: COSMONAUT

Watch as ABC reporter Jules Bergman announces Yuri Gagarin's historic flight and speaks with American astronaut John Glenn about what it means for the United States.

 ABC Bergman Glenn

After nearly an hour, Gagarin's capsule had taken him back almost to where he'd started, almost one complete orbit around Earth. With mission control guiding the Vostok, Gagarin had time to take in the experience.

He saw Earth and the stars through Vostok's tiny portholes and described the feeling of weightlessness as "pleasant and relaxing."[1]

Then, the retro-rockets fired and the craft began to spin. The instrument module had failed to separate properly, and was still attached to the reentry capsule by a cable. If the craft was unable to break free, it could be destroyed by the crushing pressure and searing temperatures of reentry. Thankfully, the cord snapped and the sphere righted itself as it plummeted through the atmosphere.

After the parachute opened, the external hatch fell away, and, with a tremendous roar, Gagarin's ejection seat shot him clear of his craft. Local villagers were startled by the parachuting man. Just 108 minutes ago, he was unknown to the world, but now he was cosmonaut Yuri Gagarin, the first person in space.

The reaction around the world was disbelief. The Soviets had bested the Americans again. Now the Soviets could boast of having put the first person in space. Headlines proclaimed the Soviet triumph, calling the accomplishment one of the most important in world history. President Kennedy, in only his third month in office, congratulated the Soviets on their success.

It was a blow to America's pride, and another embarrassing loss to their Cold War opponents. But it was about to get much worse for the new president.

The headline from Huntsville, Alabama, proclaims Gagarin's historic flight.

credit: NASA

THE BAY OF PIGS

Just days after Gagarin's flight into history, a small group of Cuban exiles launched an invasion of Cuba to drive out the communist government there. The United States had promised these rebels air support, but the air support never came, and the Bay of Pigs invasion was easily stopped by the Cuban army. Fidel Castro, Cuba's leader, was furious and turned to the USSR for help. Instead of liberating Cuba, the invasion only drove the country to side more strongly with its communist allies.

The failed effort put even more pressure on the young president. The United States' image as a powerful and prosperous nation was threatened. Was communism better at producing scientists and engineers than the West? Kennedy wanted a victory to prove the country capable of beating the Soviet system. NASA hoped it had an answer.

FREEDOM 7

In the early hours of May 5, 1961, Alan Shepard suited up and boarded *Freedom 7*, the Mercury capsule that would carry him into space. Unlike Gagarin's flight, Shepard's would be suborbital and would last a fraction of the time the Soviet cosmonaut spent circling the earth.

At 9:34 a.m., the rocket carrying America's first astronaut left its launch pad as the world watched in anticipation. The Redstone performed flawlessly, putting Shepard on a suborbital path. As *Freedom 7* rotated into position for reentry, Shepard's hands rested on the controls. Unlike Gagarin, he could control his craft.

Watch this video that combines real footage of the mission with a computer simulation to give you the entire experience! How do you think Shepard's experience of manual control made the experience different from Gagarin's flight?

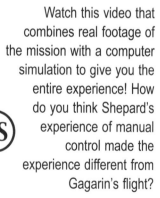

Freedom 7 full mission

Astronaut Alan Shepard, all suited up for his flight on *Freedom 7*

credit: NASA

When the capsule reached its highest altitude of 116.5 miles, Shepard was only about four and a half minutes into the flight. Even strapped to his seat, the second man in space could feel the strange sensation of weightlessness.

Minutes later, Shepard felt a jolt as the retro-rockets fired, slowing the craft as it began its fall back to Earth. Another jolt meant the parachutes deployed at the proper altitude, slowing the craft's speed even more. After 15 minutes, *Freedom 7* splashed down in the Atlantic Ocean, 300 miles from its launch pad. America had its first astronaut.

CALL OF NATURE

After spending hours of delays strapped inside the cramped spacecraft, Shepard had a problem. He radioed his fellow astronaut.

"Gordo?"

"Go, Alan."

"Man, I got to pee."

"You what?"

"You heard me, I've got to pee. I've been up here forever!"

Since Shepard's flight was to be less than 20 minutes, no waste system had been installed in the Mercury capsule. So, scientists turned off electrical equipment wired to Shepard's body and he simply peed in his suit. After he was dry, they turned everything back on and it was all systems go![2]

With Alan Shepard's successful flight, America now had the ability to put a person in space. But the two flights were very different. Vostok was a much larger and more capable craft, despite the cosmonaut having to land by parachute. And the Redstone wasn't even powerful enough to put the smaller Mercury into orbit. It was only the beginning of the Space Race, and the Soviets had a very big head start. The United States needed a win.

TO THE MOON

After the Bay of Pigs invasion and the capture of Gary Powers in the U-2 spy plane, the United States found success with the flight of Alan Shepard. Not wanting to waste the huge public support for America's early space program, President Kennedy looked for a way to show the world that America's democracy and capitalism were stronger than the communist system.

President John F. Kennedy set the goal for the Space Race on May 25, 1961. You can watch and listen to the speech at this website. Can you think of other moments in history when a presidential speech had such a resounding influence?

🔍 Kennedy Congress moon address

President John F. Kennedy, speaking to Congress May 25, 1961

credit: NASA

After consulting with Vice President Lyndon B. Johnson (1908–1973), a strong supporter of the space program, he decided that beating the Soviets in space would be a unifying goal and a demonstration of America's technological expertise. On May 25, 1961, President Kennedy gave a rousing speech to Congress, outlining America's goals to counter the communist threat.

> "First, I believe that this nation should commit itself to achieving the goal, before this decade is out, of landing a man on the moon and returning him safely to the earth. No single space project in this period will be more impressive to mankind, or more important for the long-range exploration of space; and none will be so difficult or expensive to accomplish."[3]

Suddenly, the Space Race had a finish line—the moon. Von Braun was ecstatic. His proposed Saturn rocket program would receive the necessary funding it needed to carry people to the moon, and ideally beyond. It was the challenge he had waited for since his childhood. Korolev, also aware of the finish line, remained in the shadows. But the Chief Designer had his own plans for a Soviet moon rocket.

VOCAB LAB

Write down what you think each word means. What root words can you find to help you? What does the context of the word tell you?

astronaut, **atmosphere**, **cosmonaut**, **eject**, **g-force**, **heat shield**, **mass**, **plummet**, **retro-rocket**, **surveillance**, and **vacuum**.

Compare your definitions with those of your friends or classmates. Did you all come up with the same meanings? Turn to the text and glossary if you need help.

KEY QUESTIONS

- What is the connection between politics and space exploration in each country?
- How did the Bay of Pigs incident affect relations between the two countries? How did the event highlight the suspicion that already existed?

SPLAT!

Protecting an astronaut from the dangers of space travel is a difficult task. The early spacecraft used by both space programs were small, cramped capsules designed with only one thing in mind—bringing the passenger back safely to Earth. Can you do the same? Here's your challenge: design a "space capsule" to protect a raw egg from the forces of gravity!

- **Assemble the materials you have on hand.** What can you use that could protect an egg?

- **Design your space capsule.** How will you use your materials? What is the best way to protect your "eggstronaut"?

- **Assemble your craft and test it (you can try using a hard-boiled egg first) by dropping it from shoulder height.** Make any changes needed.

- **Try dropping your capsule with its passenger from differing heights.** How does your design hold up? What is the biggest drop your eggstronaut can survive?

There are lots of ways to protect your eggstronaut! Check out this video for some ideas to ensure your intrepid explorer survives the fall!

 Incredible Science egg drop

> **To investigate more,** challenge others to a contest. Compare your strategies and designs. What materials and ideas work best?

Chapter 4 ▶
Small Steps to the Moon

THE FINISH LINE WAS TO LAND A HUMAN ON THE MOON AND RETURN THEM SAFELY TO EARTH.

Was the race to the moon worth the risk?

As both countries took more risks in the effort to land a man on the moon, the danger involved in space travel became more apparent. Even though scientists and engineers took every precaution possible, the lives of the astronauts and cosmonauts still hung in balance.

The Space Race now had the moon as its goal, but there was a lot to learn about spaceflight before anyone could step onto the lunar surface. So far, both countries had proved a person could survive in space for a short time, but a trip to the moon would take days.

Could people really survive in space that long? Could a pilot navigate the unfamiliar and unforgiving environment? How would radiation, long periods of weightlessness, and isolation affect people? The only way to find out was to keep flying.

The Soviets had put a man into orbit, while the Americans still didn't have a reliable alternative to the smaller, less-powerful Redstone. For the Americans to overcome the head start of the Soviets, the Mercury program needed to be a success.

It needed to prove that the first American in space wouldn't be the last.

GUS GRISSOM AND
LIBERTY BELL 7

Only eight weeks after President Kennedy's speech to Congress, Gus Grissom's (1926–1967) *Liberty Bell 7* roared into space on a flight meant to be a repeat of Shepard's historic trip. Grissom, an Air Force veteran and experienced test pilot, was up to the challenge.

After Shepard's trip, a few changes were made to the Mercury capsule. As requested by the astronauts, a large window was installed, giving Grissom a spectacular view. Once in space, he marveled at his view of Earth, describing it as "fascinating."[1]

More importantly, however, a new hatch with explosive bolts replaced the hand-operated one. The manual hatch took more than a minute to open, which could cost an astronaut his life in an emergency. The new hatch would open instantly with the flick of a switch.

> The hatch was far from Grissom's mind as he prepared to return to Earth.

The retro-rockets fired on schedule, slowing the craft for reentry. About 15 minutes after launch, Grissom's capsule splashed down in the Atlantic Ocean right on target. The mission was a complete success—but it wasn't over.

As Grissom prepared the capsule for recovery, he was startled by a sudden explosion. The hatch had blown without warning, quickly flooding the capsule with seawater. Still in his spacesuit, Grissom had no choice but to pull himself out of the capsule and into the choppy seas as the recovery helicopter approached.

BLAST FACT

In 1999, *Liberty Bell 7* was recovered from a depth of 15,000 feet—deeper than the *Titanic*! It is now on display at the Kansas Cosmosphere.

While the pilot tried to lift the capsule, Grissom found himself in danger of going under. Water was slowly filling his suit through an open port, and as the waves rose higher, he found it harder to keep his head above water. Fortunately, a second helicopter plucked him from the rough seas. The first helicopter had to let the capsule go. As an exhausted Grissom was taken to the recovery ship, *Liberty Bell 7* sank beneath the waves.

The dramatic rescue at sea reminded the public just how dangerous all parts of spaceflight could be. NASA had come close to losing an astronaut on just the second flight of the Mercury program, and they had yet to match the difficulty of Gagarin's flight.

Just a few weeks after Grissom's near drowning, the Soviets wowed the world with another impressive flight.

Liberty Bell 7 before it was lost beneath the waves

credit: NASA

VOSTOK 2

On August 6, 1961, it was Gherman Titov's (1935–2000) turn to make history. The second person to orbit the Earth, at 25 Titov was (and is still) the youngest person to travel in space. Although the R-7 and *Vostok 2* worked perfectly, Titov himself ran into problems. Shortly after reaching orbit, he felt as though he were tumbling, even though the capsule remained steady. Soon, nausea, dizziness, and headaches followed, making it difficult for him to complete some of his scheduled tasks.

Titov's body adapted to the strange environment. Finally able to focus, he observed through the *Vostok 2*'s portholes a view of Earth only three others before him had seen.

He ate and drank, then dozed off for a scheduled nap. After 16 revolutions around the Earth, *Vostok 2*'s retro-rockets fired. As the craft entered the atmosphere at terrific speed, the delighted cosmonaut watched through the portholes as intense heat and pressure surrounded the small sphere.

> After *Vostok 2*'s parachute opened, Titov was ejected from the capsule and parachuted to the ground. He had spent a day in orbit.

News of Titov's successful flight and landing was broadcast around the world. He'd beaten Gagarin's single orbit. He also drank, ate, and even slept in space. The Soviets were clearly far ahead of NASA.

Even though the Soviets were breaking down barriers in space, they were building them on Earth.

BLAST FACT

About half of all astronauts report feeling sick when they reach orbit. Scientists call this "space adaptation syndrome," and it is usually overcome in a matter of hours or days.

> "I had the feeling that our earth is a sand particle in the universe."
>
> —Gherman Titov, while on *Vostok 2*[2]

THE BERLIN WALL

By the beginning of 1961, 10,000 people a month fled East Berlin for West Berlin, trying to escape the worsening living conditions and oppressive East German government. Desperate to stop the loss, Moscow came up with a plan to stop the East Germans crossing the border. On the morning of August 13, just a week after Titov's ground-breaking flight, citizens from the two Berlins woke to soldiers laying the first bricks in what would become the most visible symbol of the Cold War—the Berlin Wall.

By the end of its construction, the wall stood about 12 feet tall and stretched more than 100 miles, encircling all of West Berlin. Sentry towers and land mines surrounded the wall, and guard dogs and snipers patrolled it, sometimes using deadly force to prevent anyone from the East crossing to the West.

Western nations protested the drastic move, calling on Moscow to open the border. But the East Germans, under the direction of the Soviet Union, refused. On opposite sides of the wall, American and Soviet forces faced each other across a divided city. The world watched nervously, wondering how long the stalemate could hold, and what it would take to break it.

Then, on October 30, 1961, the Soviet military detonated the largest nuclear bomb the world had ever seen. Called the Tsar Bomba, it released the energy of 50 megatons of TNT—more powerful than all the bombs and explosives used in World War II combined.

Such a weapon terrified the American people. President Kennedy urged people to build fallout shelters as schoolchildren carried out "duck-and-cover" classroom drills. Needing hope, the people of the United States looked to John Glenn.

COLD WAR FACTS

From its construction in 1961 to its demolition in 1989, the Berlin Wall stood as a symbol of the differences between East and West. About 200 people lost their lives trying to cross the closed border. The fall of the wall was celebrated on both sides of the border, and was followed by the reunification of Germany in 1990. Check out this vintage news footage from the Berlin Wall's first anniversary.

Berlin Wall first anniversary

AN AMERICAN IN ORBIT

While the Redstone booster was reliable, it was not powerful enough to reach the speed necessary to carry it around Earth. To put Glenn into orbit, NASA needed a much larger and more powerful rocket— the Air Force's Atlas missile. Atlas was America's first true ICBM, capable of delivering a nuclear warhead anywhere inside the Soviet Union. But almost half of the rocket's test launches ended in fiery explosions— not exactly the result NASA was looking for.

After a number of test flights, on November 29, 1961, an Atlas booster carried the chimpanzee Enos into orbit and his Mercury capsule brought him safely back to Earth. The Mercury-Atlas combination was declared safe, and the first American orbital flight was scheduled for early 1962.

On February 20, 1962, the world watched as John Glenn rode the Mercury-Atlas into the history books. While the rocket performed well, Glenn's Mercury capsule, *Friendship 7*, had problems as soon as he reached orbit. Automatic systems that controlled the craft's positioning failed, requiring the astronaut to take over. For the experienced pilot, this wasn't a problem. But, unknown to Glenn, something more serious was making mission control very worried. As he circled the earth, a warning light indicated that *Friendship 7*'s heat shield was loose. Those on the ground knew that if the heat shield failed, Glenn wouldn't survive the intense heat of reentry.

Mission control decided not to tell Glenn about the warning light, instead instructing him that the retro-rockets would remain strapped to the bottom of the craft for reentry. Once used, the retro-rockets were usually discarded, but engineers hoped they would hold the heat shield in place.

During the Cold War, schoolchildren practiced duck-and-cover drills to prepare for a nuclear attack. Check out this video used to teach children to how to duck and cover.

duck and cover video

On November 29, 1961, a chimpanzee named Enos became the first primate to orbit Earth. His successful Mercury-Atlas flight proved the more powerful Atlas rocket was safe, and paved the way for John Glenn's historic launch.

John Glenn and his *Friendship 7* capsule

credit: NASA

BLACKOUT

During reentry, a craft's incredible speed though the thickening atmosphere creates so much friction that the molecules of gas become a plasma. Radio waves can't penetrate this form of matter, so every spacecraft returning to Earth experiences a blackout period when no communication is possible. It's always a tense time for those on the ground!

After completing three orbits, the retro-rockets fired and *Friendship 7*'s fall back to Earth began. It was a tense moment for everyone as they waited to hear from Glenn. Nobody was sure if the heat shield would hold or if America's first astronaut in orbit would also be the first astronaut to die. After five long minutes of radio silence, Glenn's voice crackled over the speakers at mission control.

CapCom: How do you read? Over.
Friendship 7: Loud and clear

Mission control, along with the entire country, breathed a sigh of relief. America finally had a flight to rival the Soviet Union, and Glenn was given star treatment. Millions lined the streets of New York City to watch him and his fellow astronauts in a parade as ticker tape rained down.

In a speech to Congress, Glenn stated that the United States was committed to peaceful and open exploration of space. He pointed out that the American space program was conducted openly and in front of the world. Although he didn't name the Soviet Union, it was clear that Glenn believed the secrecy around their rocket program did little to lessen the tensions of the Cold War.

SCIENCE IN SPACE

After the nationwide celebration of John Glenn's orbital flight, attention turned to Scott Carpenter (1925–2013) and his *Aurora 7* spacecraft. The first three launches satisfied NASA that the Mercury capsule could keep an astronaut safe, and it was now time to start doing more research on the scientific and practical effects of spaceflight.

If the United States was to land on the moon, a number of questions had to be answered. How would fluids behave in space? How could a pilot navigate a spacecraft? Before Carpenter's flight, astronauts had eaten only nutritional paste squeezed from a tube. What would happen if an astronaut ate solid food? To answer these questions, Scott Carpenter's *Aurora 7* lifted off on May 24, 1962.

Once in orbit, Carpenter began his experiments. He took pictures of Earth's horizon to help design a navigation system to take astronauts to the moon. Maneuvering the capsule proved to be easy and fun for the new astronaut. But the solid, freeze-dried "food cubes" turned to crumbs during launch, making them a danger to the delicate instruments. Even the candy bar he was given melted from the heat in the cramped cabin. Despite the disappointing snacks, Carpenter enjoyed the ride and the magnificent view of Earth below.

Scott Carpenter inside the *Aurora 7* Mercury capsule

credit: NASA

After five orbits, Carpenter prepared the capsule for reentry. While putting *Aurora 7* into the correct position, he discovered that the system used to change the pitch of the craft had malfunctioned. He was suddenly very low on the fuel needed to keep his ship lined up properly for reentry. Without the correct positioning, the capsule could burn up as it plummeted through the atmosphere. Luckily, the capsule's design allowed it to right itself as it fell. *Aurora 7* splashed down safely in the Atlantic, although 250 miles from the intended landing zone.

Carpenter had fired the retro-rockets late, distracted by the problems with pitch and fuel. As the recovery ships steamed toward him, news reports declared NASA had "lost" an astronaut at sea, and that the military was combing the ocean to find him.

Millions tuned in to wait for
the astronaut's rescue.

Thankfully, Carpenter and his capsule were picked up about three hours after splashdown. The newest astronaut was found floating comfortably in his life raft.

It seemed the Americans were about to move ahead in the Space Race. However, the Soviets weren't willing to give up their lead.

A RENDEZVOUS IN SPACE

On August 11, 1962, cosmonaut Andriyan Nikolayev (1929–2004) left the Baikonur Cosmodrome aboard *Vostok 3*. The West assumed it was a repeat of the *Vostok 2* flight and expected to hear little from the secretive Soviets. However, the launch of Pavel Popovich in *Vostok 4* the very next day had the entire world paying attention to the Soviets once again.

The liftoff was perfectly timed to
meet up with Nikolayev in *Vostok 3*—
the first rendezvous in space.

Soviet television broadcasts showed the joyous
pilots floating free in their cabins, a first for manned
spaceflight. The cosmonauts performed experiments
and even signaled to one another over radio.
Vostok 3 spent nearly four days in orbit, while
Vostok 4 stayed up for almost three days. It was an
impressive, record-setting pair of missions.

While the Soviet accomplishment was stunning,
it wasn't quite what it appeared. In fact, Vostok
capsules weren't able to change their orbits, as many
at NASA assumed. The timing of the *Vostok 4* launch
allowed the two craft to come within four miles of
each other, but with only small maneuvering rockets,
they quickly drifted apart in space. The Soviets were
happy to let the United States believe otherwise,
and Khrushchev was very pleased with the results.

THE PERFECT FLIGHT

Once again in the shadow of the Soviets, NASA had
no choice but to press on with more Mercury flights.
The orbital rendezvous was a difficult feat to follow.
The task fell to Navy pilot Wally Schirra (1923–2007).
Schirra was an excellent choice for a mission that
would push the limits of his *Sigma 7* craft.

A smooth October 3, 1962, launch on an Atlas
booster put Wally Schirra in a near-perfect orbit.
Right away, he got to work testing newly designed
thrusters and *Sigma 7*'s navigation systems. He
proved that a pilot could navigate precisely in space
using only the earth and stars, an important step in
flying to the moon.

If the reports were
true, the Soviets'
ability to maneuver
and rendezvous in
space was way ahead
of anything Project
Mercury could do.
How could the
United States beat
them to the moon?

You can watch President Kennedy's Oval Office address during the Cuban Missile Crisis at this website. How does President Kennedy's language compare to the language politicians use today?

🔍 C-Span
Kennedy Cuban

During his nine-hour flight, Schirra tested the electrical and life-support systems to work out emergency routines if a capsule were to lose power. Once the testing was finished, Schirra fired the retro-rockets and returned to Earth, completing the most successful and problem-free Mercury flight yet. It was so successful, in fact, that NASA decided to speed up the program and go ahead with an even longer mission for the final Mercury flight. But only days after Schirra's successful mission, a new and frightening development in the Cold War threatened to end the race to the moon, and even all life on Earth.

NUCLEAR CRISIS

After the disastrous Bay of Pigs invasion, Cuba's communist leader, Fidel Castro, asked the Soviet Union for help defending the island from American aggression. Secretly, Soviet politician Nikita Khrushchev approved the shipment of nuclear missiles to the island nation, placing them just 103 miles from the Florida coast. American spies in Cuba noticed strange shipments arriving, and a U-2 spy plane confirmed the U.S. government's suspicions.

Many of President Kennedy's advisors urged him to invade, hoping to rid the island of both the nuclear threat and communism in one blow. Only a month before, the Soviet government had promised the buildup in Cuba was only defensive, and that their superior R-7 missile technology made putting nuclear missiles close to the United States unnecessary. The nuclear arms in Cuba were a violation of that promise, and threatened to turn the Cold War into a hot one.

On October 22, 1962, President Kennedy addressed the American people by radio and television. Instead of an invasion, he declared a naval blockade of Cuba.

Unlike the Soviet blockade of West Berlin, the Americans would allow food and goods to pass, but no weapons. President Kennedy promised that if the Soviets did not remove their nuclear missiles from Cuba, the United States would take further action. And if a missile was launched toward any nation in the Western Hemisphere, it would be considered an attack on the United States, and the United States would respond in kind. Kennedy sent a clear message that Americans would not tolerate Soviet missiles so close to home— but nobody was sure how Moscow would respond.

It was a tense and terrifying time, not just in the United States, but around the world. With both militaries on highest alert, a wrong move at any moment could start the next world war. Although it was always known that the technology used to send men to space was the same technology that could cause a nuclear war, it was never clearer than at the end of 1962. Were the rockets the astronauts and cosmonauts rode really about peaceful exploration of space or had the Space Race set the stage for nuclear war?

The first photo that showed Soviet missiles located in Cuba

credit: U.S. Air Force

REMEMBERING THE CUBAN MISSILE CRISIS

Can you imagine what it was like to live through the Cuban Missile Crisis? Click the link below to listen to two people describe what it was like for them. One was in Florida and the other was in Cuba!

🔍 NPR childhood missile

Finally, Khrushchev agreed to remove the nuclear missiles in exchange for the United States' secret pledge to not invade Cuba. By the end of November, the Soviets had removed their missiles and the Cuban Missile Crisis was over, though tensions remained high. Having come so close to a nuclear war, both leaders looked for ways to calm the level of mistrust between the two nations.

On April 5, 1963, the United States and Soviet Union agreed to a "hotline," a direct phone connection between Washington, DC, and Moscow, to avoid such conflicts in the future. It signaled a warming between the two nations, one that both Kennedy and Khrushchev hoped would lead to a better relationship.

THE END OF PROJECT MERCURY

On May 15, 1963, the Space Race continued with the final flight of Project Mercury. Following the success of Wally Schirra's mission, astronaut Gordon Cooper's (1927–2004) mission was to be the longest of the Mercury program, finally demonstrating that NASA could keep a person alive in space for more than a few hours. It would push Cooper and his capsule, *Faith 7*, to the limit.

After an uneventful launch, Cooper performed several experiments, including tracking a small beacon detached from *Faith 7* and photographing Earth's surface. With a short nap, Cooper became the first American to sleep in space after his 10th orbit. But after the 20th orbit, his capsule was showing some signs of wear. A short circuit left the automatic stabilization system without electrical power, and Cooper was unable to get any position readings from his instruments. Worse, the carbon dioxide levels in his suit were rising.

BROKEN HEART

Although chosen as one of the Mercury Seven, Deke Slayton (1924–1993) never rode a Mercury capsule into orbit. Doctors discovered a heart condition that could have been fatal during spaceflight and he was grounded. Not one to give up, Slayton remained with NASA and was finally able to reach space in 1975.

Gordon Cooper after the final flight of Project Mercury

credit: NASA

Despite mounting problems, Cooper persevered. To properly turn the craft, Cooper drew lines on the window and lined them up with familiar constellations. Using his wristwatch, he timed the firing of his retro-rockets perfectly and landed just four miles from his recovery ship in an amazing display of skill and preparation. It was a fitting end to NASA's first spaceflight program, and cleared the way for a much more ambitious program called Gemini.

As the United States wrapped up the Mercury program, the USSR was nearing the end of the Vostok program. But before it concluded, the Chief Designer had a few more surprises for the world.

THE HAWK AND THE SEAGULL

It had been almost a year since the stunning dual *Vostok 3* and *Vostok 4* missions, and the West wondered what the Soviets would do next. A month after the final Mercury flight, on June 14, cosmonaut Valery Bykovsky (1934–) rode into orbit aboard *Vostok 5*.

> Would the Soviets try another rendezvous in orbit? Or was something different planned?

With the call sign Yastreb ("Hawk"), the new cosmonaut was scheduled for a record-setting eight-day mission performing navigation and zero-gravity experiments, as well as an orbital rendezvous with *Vostok 6*. With a launch timed to meet up with *Vostok 5*, *Vostok 6*'s June 16 liftoff confirmed Western suspicions.

Although the launch of *Vostok 6* wasn't a surprise, its passenger was. Through the government-run media, Moscow announced another Soviet-first: Valentina Tereshkova (1937–), with the call sign Chayka ("Seagull"), was the first woman in space.

What about women in the United States? Why had men dominated the space program so far? Actually, there were women involved in a privately funded program. Known as the First Lady Astronaut Trainees (FLATs, or the Mercury 13), these women were all exceptional pilots with an interest in the space program. Despite passing many of the same physical and mental tests as the men, they were denied the chance to continue testing when a congressional hearing decided it wouldn't change NASA's selection criteria, which excluded anyone who did not graduate from an Air Force training school.

The first American woman in space, Sally Ride (1951–2012), wouldn't get her chance until 1983.

BLAST FACT

Both John Glenn and Scott Carpenter testified against admitting women into the program.

The Soviet Union, however, wanted to show the world that communism treated men and women equally by sending a female into space. Valentina Tereshkova was fascinated with space travel, and was eventually chosen from dozens of candidates in a secret, nationwide search. Unlike the male cosmonauts, Tereshkova wasn't a member of the military and had no flying experience. But she was an amateur parachutist and a devoted member of the Communist Party, both useful qualities for the Soviet government and space program.

Like the FLATs, the female candidates in the Soviet Union faced sexism from many of their male countrymen. Of the final four women, Tereshkova was selected as the first female cosmonaut. There wouldn't be another one for nearly 20 years, until Svetlana Savitskaya (1948–) in 1982.

With Tereshkova's launch, the Soviet Union claimed another first. Soviet newspapers declared their society provided equal opportunity for everyone, while the Americans seemed to think only men were capable of space flight. The safe return of both cosmonauts was followed by triumphant celebrations of the newest Soviet heroes across the country. The first leg of the Space Race was over, with the Soviets again in the lead in the eyes of the world.

1963 postage stamp featuring Valentina Tereshkova

To learn more about the FLATs, read the article at this website. How have attitudes toward women changed since the 1960s?

🔍 Popsci Mercury 13

KEY QUESTIONS

- **The astronauts had to request larger windows in their space capsules. Why do you think engineers didn't think of this in the initial designs?**

- **Do you think gender equality is better today than it was in the United States in the 1960s?**

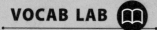

Inquire & Investigate

VOCAB LAB

Write down what you think each word means. What root words can you find to help you? What does the context of the word tell you?

constellation, friction, hatch, mission control, nausea, plasma, rendezvous, sexism, short circuit, and **stalemate.**

Compare your definitions with those of your friends or classmates. Did you all come up with the same meanings? Turn to the text and glossary if you need help.

THE EDGE OF DISASTER

In the fall of 1962, the Cuban Missile Crisis brought the world to the edge of nuclear war. During that time, most Americans knew very little about what was happening behind the scenes between the United States and the Soviet Union. What was really going on?

- **Create a two-part timeline of the Cuban Missile Crisis.**

- **What did the public know?** Research newspaper articles or television broadcasts during the days of the missile crisis.

- **What was going on behind the scenes?** Look at what President Kennedy and other members of the government knew and how they responded.

- **Compare the two timelines.** Questions to consider include the following.

  - How much did the public really know at the time?

  - What important information was kept secret, and why?

  - Do you think the public would have reacted differently had it known what the government knew?

  - Was it reasonable to keep some of the facts from the public, and why or why not?

> **To investigate more,** speak with someone who remembers the missile crisis. How much did they know at the time, and what did they think and feel in October 1962? Do they feel differently now that the details of the events are better known?

Chapter 5 ▶
America Takes the Lead

WHY DID AMERICA TAKE ALMOST A DECADE TO GET TO THE MOON?

How did the United States manage to pull ahead in the Space Race?

Despite many setbacks, the United States kept its commitment to the space program and encouraged the scientists and engineers at NASA to come up with new ways of exploring space.

Tensions between the United States and the USSR remained high. The Cuban Missile Crisis demonstrated just how dangerous the Cold War could be. To prevent the accidental start of nuclear war, the two nations had agreed to establish a hotline in April 1963. The hope was that future emergencies could be dealt with better if the two nations could reach each other immediately. There was much more than national pride at stake.

At the same time, since construction of the Berlin Wall in 1961, Eastern Europe had become more isolated than ever.

A determined President Kennedy decided to visit West Berlin to reassure European allies that the United States, despite seemingly behind in space and missile technology, was firmly committed and able to defend Western Europe.

On June 26, 1963, President Kennedy gave a passionate speech to nearly half a million West Germans in West Berlin. In his famous "Ich bin ein Berliner" address, he pledged "I am a Berliner," declaring America's solidarity with West Germany and Western Europe. He scolded the Soviet Union, saying: "Democracy is not perfect, but we have not had to put a wall up to keep our people in." The Soviets still considered Berlin to be part of East Germany, and an American president supporting this outpost of Western democracy was not well received.[1]

COOPERATION

Despite Kennedy's speech, both nations spent much of 1963 seeking ways to slow the growing number of nuclear weapons and their dangerous tests. In August, the United States, United Kingdom, and USSR signed the Limited Test Ban Treaty, ending the detonation of nuclear weapons in the atmosphere, beneath the ocean, and in space.

Encouraged, Kennedy addressed the United Nations that fall and called for more cooperation between the two nations—including a joint mission to the moon. Kennedy wasn't proposing a joint mission simply for peaceful reasons. The cost of winning the Space Race would be incredibly high, and many people saw it as a waste of money and resources that could be better spent elsewhere. The president had considered ending the program, or at least scaling back America's efforts.

The Soviets were also aware of the cost of the race, and committing huge amounts of their military's money for national prestige did not sit well with many in the Kremlin. Sharing the costs and risk might be the answer for both governments.

You can listen to President Kennedy's "I am a Berliner" speech at this website. How did his words affect the relationship between the United States and the USSR?

Kennedy Berliner speech

BLAST FACT

In announcing his hopes for the Limited Test Ban Treaty at American University on June 10, 1963, Kennedy said: "If we cannot end now our differences, at least we can help make the world safe for diversity. For, in the final analysis, our most basic common link is that we all inhabit this small planet. We all breathe the same air. We all cherish our children's future. And we are all mortal."[2]

There was some interest from Khrushchev, but before any decisions could be made, talk of cooperation between the two powers ended with the tragic events in Dallas, Texas.

THE DEATH OF A PRESIDENT

The morning of November 22, 1963, a crowd of more than 150,000 people gathered to see the president and his wife make their way through downtown Dallas. But as the motorcade went by, the excited cheers were interrupted by the sound of gunfire. President Kennedy and Texas Governor John Connally (1917–1993) were both shot as their car drove through Dealey Plaza. Just an hour later, it was officially announced that President Kennedy had died.

After the swearing in of Vice President Lyndon B. Johnson, Nikita Khrushchev expressed his condolences to the new president and the American people. The United States, and much of the world, was in mourning.

President Kennedy, moments before he was assassinated in Dallas, Texas, 1963

credit: Victor Hugo King

With the loss of President Kennedy, some Americans wondered if the space program would continue. But Kennedy's commitment was a part of his legacy, one that President Johnson intended to honor.

At NASA, work progressed on Gemini, the second human spaceflight program. A successful, un-crewed test in April 1964 of Gemini and its new booster, the Titan II missile, told the world that the Americans were still in the race. Meanwhile, Korolev and his team worked on Soyuz, the next Soviet manned spacecraft.

Khrushchev was eager to keep the Soviet lead in space. He demanded that Korolev send up a crew of three cosmonauts before the two-person Gemini could get off the ground. Under pressure from Moscow, Korolev hatched a simple but dangerous plan.

VOSKHOD 1

To beat Gemini, the Soyuz program was put on hold. Instead, the Soviets returned to the craft that had successfully beaten the Americans several times. Vostok was roomy on the inside, but was meant to carry only one cosmonaut. Korolev set to work turning Vostok into a craft called Voskhod.

Engineers decided to remove the ejection seats to make space for three cosmonauts. While this also meant less weight, there would be no safe exit during the first few minutes after launch. Landing rockets were added to allow the crew to ride the craft all the way to the ground. Additionally, the bulky spacesuits would be left behind. If Voskhod lost pressure, the cosmonauts would not survive long in space.

> To be first, Moscow was willing to accept these risks.

BLAST FACT

At the time, the cost of getting to the moon reached about $10 billion, which would be about $100 billion today!

Khrushchev's removal from power seemed sudden in the West, but many members of the Soviet government had been planning his ouster for a long time. Khrushchev made a number of very public blunders that embarrassed the government, including a disastrous attempt to grow corn. But his handling of the Cuban Missile Crisis was likely the last straw. Being forced to remove the missiles from Cuba was a huge setback for the Soviets that led to his peaceful "retirement" from office. Despite his success with the early space program, he was the only Soviet leader not to be buried within the Kremlin after his death.

In October, the crash course to turn Vostok into Voskhod paid off when three cosmonauts rocketed into orbit stuffed tightly into their *Voskhod 1* capsule. Piloted by Vladimir Komarov (1927–1967), the crew also included spacecraft engineer Konstantin Feoktistov (1926–2009) and flight doctor Boris Yegorov (1937–1994).

It was a short flight. With three crew members, the craft could carry only enough supplies for one day in space, and after 16 trips around the earth, *Voskhod 1* returned safely to Earth. Publicizing the "new" ship, Khrushchev praised the crew and its designers. To the world, Voskhod seemed to be a brand-new craft capable of much more than the still-in-progress Gemini. The Soviets always seemed to be one step ahead, anticipating what the Americans would do and beating them to it.

As Khrushchev celebrated the success of *Voskhod 1* from his vacation home, things were moving quickly in Moscow. Many in the Kremlin were unhappy with Khrushchev's leadership, and wanted a change. Almost a year after the death of President Kennedy, in October 1964, a group of Communist Party leaders removed Khrushchev from his post as premier. Promising greater prosperity and a de-escalation of hostility with the West, Leonid Brezhnev (1906–1982) became the new leader of the USSR.

VIETNAM HEATS UP

Despite the sudden change in Soviet leadership, the Cold War remained outwardly calm. Many hoped that the Space Race would remain the only source of competition between the two nations, but another conflict in Southeast Asia threatened to turn the world back toward war.

Like Korea, the country of Vietnam was divided between the communist North and the non-communist South. Since the late 1950s, the U.S. military had sent thousands of advisors to Vietnam, helping to train the South Vietnamese army to fight the Soviet- and Chinese-supported North. In March 1965, the first American combat forces arrived in Vietnam. It was a dramatic escalation. Brezhnev was outraged at the arrival of American troops, stating that their presence threatened to start a larger war.

Unhappy with the president's decision, many anti-war protests broke out across the United States. But President Johnson was unwilling to back down.

GOING FOR A WALK

Just weeks after the escalation in Vietnam, *Voskhod 2* left the Baikonur Cosmodrome, prepared to make history. Instead of three tightly packed passengers, it carried only two—Pavel Belyayev (1925–1970) and Alexey Leonov (1934–). Without the third cosmonaut, *Voskhod 2* could support its crew a little longer, but this wasn't the goal of the mission. Attached to the outside of the craft was an inflatable airlock, designed to let a person leave the safety of the capsule and float freely in space.

As *Voskhod 2* started its second orbit, the airlock was extended from the craft. Air filled the small chamber, equalizing pressure between it and the capsule. Leonov, protected in his spacesuit, floated into the airlock, while Belyayev closed the hatch behind him.

> Once all the air was removed from the tunnel, Leonov floated out of the airlock and into open space.

The airlock from *Voskhod 2*, now at the Memorial Museum of Astronautics in Moscow

credit: Armael

He was attached to his spacecraft by a long cable that kept him from drifting away from his ticket back to Earth. Psychologists had worried that a person might not be able to handle the experience of floating alone in space, but Leonov was mesmerized. He was fascinated by everything he experienced—the heat of the sun, the blackness of space, and the earth below. He was the first person to perform a spacewalk, and he loved it.

> Getting out of the *Voskhod 2* capsule was easy, but getting back in proved to be much more dangerous.

During his spacewalk, Leonov's spacesuit had puffed up like a balloon, making it hard for him to move. Worse, he was now much too big to fit through the airlock. He was exhausted from fighting his suit, and if he couldn't find a way in, he would be stranded outside as day turned to night. He had to reduce the pressure in his suit.

Without informing mission control, he slowly allowed air to escape from a valve. If he let out too much, bubbles could form in his blood and kill him, a condition deep-sea divers call the bends. Fortunately, he squeezed into the capsule before he lost consciousness.

Back on Earth, Moscow broadcast the historic achievement, with Brezhnev praising Leonov's performance and bravery. NASA had yet to fly a Gemini mission, and the Soviets had stretched their lead in the Space Race even further. Many critics complained that at this rate, there would be a Soviet flag on the moon long before an American one. For the Soviets, Leonov's triumph marked an end to the successful Vostok/Voskhod program.

Alexey Leonov's historic spacewalk was a turning point for spaceflight, proving that people could survive outside a spacecraft. You can watch footage of Leonov's spacewalk here. Why was reporting such a significant part of traveling in space on these early missions? Is it as important today?

🔍 first spacewalk video

· · · · · · · · · · · · · · · · · · · ·

Nobody on Earth knew how close Alexey Leonov had been to being the first man to die in orbit.

BACK IN SPACE

On March 23, 1965, America was back in the Space Race as *Gemini 3* carried Gus Grissom and John Young (1930–2018) into orbit. *Gemini 3* was a shakedown mission, a short flight to test the craft's systems. During their five-hour flight, Grissom and Young managed to change the size and shape of *Gemini 3's* orbit, a first for a spacecraft and a major goal of the program. With a successful splashdown, *Gemini 3* was the first in a rapid series of Gemini launches that put America firmly on the path to the moon.

Three months after *Gemini 3*, *Gemini 4* lofted Ed White (1930–1967) and Jim McDivitt (1929–) into orbit for a four-day flight packed with difficult and dangerous goals. First, *Gemini 4* was to rendezvous with the upper stage of its Titan II booster as it drifted after them. But judging distance by eye turned out to be much harder than expected, and the astronauts quickly ran out of time. The most anticipated and dangerous part of the mission was about to begin.

Gus Grissom and John Young

credit: NASA/MSFC archives

BLAST FACT

Leonov and Belyayev's harrowing adventure didn't end with the spacewalk. The two cosmonauts landed more than 236 miles off course in a frozen, remote area. They spent two nights in the wolf- and bear-infested countryside before heading out with their rescue teams—on skis!

On their third orbit, Ed White pushed open the hatch over his seat. With the Pacific Ocean gliding beneath him, he stood up and used a small "zip gun" of compressed air to push himself away from *Gemini 4*. Like Leonov, White was awed by the magnificent view and the feeling of floating in empty space. After more than 20 minutes, White reluctantly returned to *Gemini 4*, calling it the saddest moment of his life.

Ed White's spacewalk proved that the U.S. space program was capable of matching the Soviet achievements. With Soyuz delayed, Korolev could only watch as the Americans began moving ahead.

EIGHT DAYS IN A GARBAGE CAN

The first time the United States could claim a true first in space was with *Gemini 5*. Gordon Cooper (1927–2004) and Pete Conrad (1930–1999) spent seven days and 22 hours in their cramped capsule, breaking the Soviet endurance record and demonstrating that people could survive in space long enough to make it to the moon and back.

They also tested new electrical and navigation systems meant for travel to the moon, and performed medical tests to monitor their health during the long mission. After the mission, Conrad joked that he wished he'd brought a book with him to read during "eight days in a garbage can."

Jim Lovell (1928–) and Frank Borman (1928–) followed Conrad's advice, and brought books along for their *Gemini 7* mission. Lifting off on December 4, 1965, for almost two weeks in orbit, their trip was even longer than *Gemini 5*. But before they returned to Earth, Wally Schirra and Thomas Stafford (1930–) headed up to meet them aboard *Gemini 6A*.

Once in orbit, Schirra and Stafford tracked *Gemini 7* using radar, another first. Soon, the two capsules could see each other, and managed to fly as close as 1 foot apart. Unlike the Vostok rendezvous, the two Gemini capsules could stay together instead of drifting apart, and could have docked with each other if they'd had the right equipment.

Gemini was a huge success. NASA flew five missions in just nine months, an amazing feat on its own, with no flights from the Soviets. The Americans had performed a spacewalk, changed orbit, made a rendezvous, and shattered the record for longest spaceflight. All the while, the Soviet Cosmodrome was silent.

For the first time, the United States seemed ahead in the race to the moon. But would it last?

FAREWELL TO THE CHIEF DESIGNER

With the United States' Gemini program making progress at an incredible rate, Korolev was under pressure to provide a Soviet answer. The Soyuz spacecraft he hoped would take cosmonauts to the moon was still behind schedule, and the stress affected his health.

On January 14, 1966, Sergei Korolev died from complications in surgery. Korolev was finally revealed to the world as the architect behind *Sputnik* and the man who put the first person in space. He received a hero's burial at the Kremlin, with his cosmonauts and Leonid Brezhnev in attendance. The death of the Chief Designer was a blow to space exploration, and had a devastating impact on the Soviets' efforts to beat the United States to the moon. He left behind a huge amount of unfinished work, something his successor, Vasily Mishin (1917–2001), inherited, including Korolev's secret, massive moon rocket, the N-1.

BLAST FACT

In 1996, the Russian city of Kaliningrad was renamed Korolev to honor the accomplishments of the Chief Designer. Today, it is home to many parts of the Russian space program, managed by an agency called Roscosmos.

EMERGENCY IN ORBIT

With the brilliant successes of 1965, NASA's *Gemini 8* mission was expected to mark another successful milestone on the way to the moon. After their March 16, 1966, launch, astronauts David Scott (1932–) and Neil Armstrong (1930–2012) got to work on *Gemini 8*'s main goal: docking with the unmanned Agena target craft. The crew located its target quickly and docked successfully, another U.S. first. But after linking together, the ships began rolling. As the rate of the roll increased, mission control directed the astronauts to pull away from Agena, suspecting the problem was with the unmanned vehicle.

> Once undocked, however, the spinning got much worse.

Armstrong and Scott began to feel dizzy and nauseous, finding it hard to read their instruments. The astronauts were in danger of blacking out. Finally, Armstrong managed to turn off the reaction control system and stop the roll manually. But with almost all of the fuel needed to orient *Gemini 8* for reentry used up, mission control ordered an emergency return to Earth. After just 10 hours in space, *Gemini 8* splashed down safely, an uncomfortable reminder of the dangers of spaceflight.

Despite the setback, the pace of Gemini flights only increased. In June, *Gemini 9* lifted off to try another rendezvous and docking with an Agena, as well as a second American spacewalk. But when Gene Cernan (1934–2017) and Thomas Stafford approached, they could see that the docking mechanism hadn't opened. The docking was called off, and the next phase of the mission began.

SILVER LININGS

Despite problems, *Gemini 9A* was still considered a success. Cernan's fogged visor led to the development of a liquid-cooled spacesuit that would help keep sweating to a minimum, and the near-perfect landing was the first that was controlled completely by an onboard computer. Both were crucial steps in the race to the moon.

When Cernan stepped out of his seat for his spacewalk, he felt the same awe that Alexey Leonov and Ed White had before him. But instead of just floating about, Cernan was assigned tasks to perform to see how well a human could actually work in space.

Almost from the beginning, he had trouble. As with Leonov, his suit stiffened up from air pressure, making it extremely hard to move around. As he strained to work, his visor started to fog from his sweat, making it hard to see. The rest of the spacewalk was called off, and an exhausted Cernan was glad to return to his spacecraft, and to Earth.

Cernan's view from his spacewalk

credit: NASA

THE END OF GEMINI

Gemini's final three flights completed all of the program's main goals. The flight of *Gemini 10* in July of 1966 saw John Young (1930–2018) and Michael Collins (1930–) perform a double rendezvous, finally docking successfully with an Agena and using its engine to meet with another target vehicle. Two successful spacewalks by Collins capped the short but successful three-day flight.

In September, *Gemini 11* continued *Gemini 10*'s success. Dick Gordon (1929–2017) performed two strenuous spacewalks, and Pete Conrad (1930–1999) used a docked Agena engine to raise their orbit to a record 850 miles above Earth.

The final Gemini mission on November 11, 1966, with Buzz Aldrin (1930–) and Jim Lovell put America firmly in the lead of the Space Race. Although they were unable to use an Agena booster, Aldrin performed three successful spacewalks, conducting experiments and taking pictures. Their splashdown on November 15 was the end of the hugely successful Gemini program.

The knowledge gained about navigation, long-duration spaceflight, and working in space provided NASA with the tools they needed to go for the moon with Project Apollo.

BLAST FACT

Among the experiments carried out by *Gemini 11* was an attempt to generate artificial gravity by spinning the Agena and Gemini capsules together on a cable. They managed to generate a small force, just 0.00015 times the force of gravity on Earth.

KEY QUESTIONS

- How does a change in leadership affect both a country's politics and its ability to advance in the sciences?
- How might the vision of Earth from space change a person's perception of our planet?

COMPARE AND CONTRAST

The early space programs of Mercury, Gemini, Vostok, and Voskhod formed the foundations for space travel. How were the programs alike and how were they different?

- **Compare and contrast the American and Soviet early spacecraft.** For example, you can make lists, create a diagram, or design a poster.

- **How did the Soviets' use of secrecy both help and hurt their efforts in the Space Race?** How did it affect the American program and NASA's decisions?

- **Despite the rhetoric of the Cold War, astronauts and cosmonauts shared many experiences.** Research the space explorers from both nations. Some questions to think about include the following.

  - What were they like?

  - How did they describe the effect of space travel on their lives?

  - Did they see each other as enemies, friends, or something else?

> **To investigate more,** compare the space programs of the world today. Is there competition between nations, or do they cooperate? Is there still a "space race" happening today?

VOCAB LAB

Write down what you think each word means. What root words can you find to help you? What does the context of the word tell you?

airlock, de-escalation, escalation, Kremlin, legacy, mesmerized, navigation, prestige, radar, radioactive, and **solidarity.**

Compare your definitions with those of your friends or classmates. Did you all come up with the same meanings? Turn to the text and glossary if you need help.

TO THE MOON!

President Kennedy's speech calling for an American on the moon was an inspirational challenge to the country. But Kennedy himself had limited interest in space exploration.

- **Do some research into President Kennedy and his personal interests.** What was Kennedy's motivation in giving such a speech, if he didn't feel as strongly about space as historians believe?

- **Without a presidential directive to go to the moon before the end of the 1960s, do you think it would have happened?**
  - Why or why not?
  - How might history have been different if another president had led the country during those years?

- **Create a presentation to show how today might have been different had President Kennedy not been the leader of the country in the 1960s.**

To investigate more, consider how history might have fared had President Kennedy not been assassinated. What would have been different? What might relations have been like between the United States and the Soviet Union?

Chapter 6 ▶
Crossing the Finish Line

WOULD WE HAVE EVER LANDED ON THE MOON IF IT WASN'T FOR THE COLD WAR? SHOULD WE SAY THANK YOU?

Would humans have reached the moon if not for the Cold War?

The competition between the United States and the Soviet Union spurred both countries to make major strides in the science and technology needed to reach the moon. Today, scientists are still looking to the stars and beyond, and cooperation is more typical than competition.

The year 1966 was the U.S. space program's finest. Project Gemini accomplished all its tasks, helping NASA prepare to put an American on the moon. Project Apollo was the result of lessons learned from the Mercury and Gemini missions. NASA had the knowledge and experience it needed to take America to the moon.

Although it shared a background with the earlier spacecraft, Apollo was bigger and more complex than anything that had ever flown. It consisted of two spacecraft: the command and service module and the lunar module. The command module would carry three astronauts to the moon and back, splashing down safely in the ocean. The lunar module was designed to take two of the astronauts to the moon, and return them to the command module for the trip home.

Both modules would ride on top of the most powerful rocket in the world—the Saturn V.

THE U.S. MONSTER ROCKET

To meet President Kennedy's challenge of putting a man on the moon and returning him safely to Earth, von Braun would have to design the largest rocket the world had ever seen.

Throughout the Mercury and Gemini programs, von Braun worked on the giant Saturn V as the Soviets first led the Space Race and then fell behind. Such a large and complicated rocket took years to develop. At the time, it was the most complex machine the United States had ever built.

Despite the lead that Gemini had given NASA, to make sure the United States was first to the moon, the Saturn V and its three stages would have to be tested all at once, a plan von Braun opposed. Usually, each stage of a rocket was tested on its own before it was joined with the others. An all-up test could save months or even years—if it worked.

It was a risky idea, one that could delay or even destroy America's best chance at beating the Soviets and their secret rocket.

THE SOVIET MONSTER ROCKET

With Sergei Korolev's death, the Soviet space program faced a crisis. Korolev was known for his ability to bring complex and intricate ideas into a single, useful vision. Now it was up to Vasily Mishin to pull together the Soviet's mega-rocket, the N-1.

BLAST FACT

At 363 feet tall and 6.2 million pounds, the Saturn V is still the largest rocket ever to fly. Capable of generating 7.6 million pounds of thrust, it could put 130 tons into orbit, or send 50 tons to the moon.

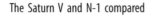
The Saturn V and N-1 compared

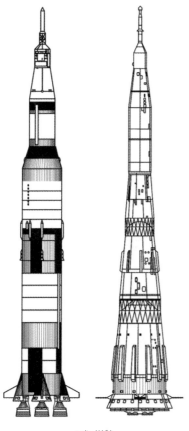
credit: NASA

Korolev began work on the massive rocket in the early 1960s. Designed with the same goal, the N-1 and Saturn V were very different rockets. In the first stage alone, the N-1 had a complicated cluster of 30 small rocket engines, while the Saturn V first stage had just five huge engines. The other four stages of the N-1 also contained smaller and smaller clusters of rockets, making the control system extremely complex.[1]

It was the kind of work that the former Chief Designer excelled at, but with Korolev gone, Mishin faced the challenges of finishing his mentor's rocket in secrecy. If the Soviets were to send cosmonauts to the moon, the N-1 needed to be a success.

APOLLO I

With the Saturn V's first all-up test scheduled for the end of 1967, testing of the spacecraft it would carry was already underway. Mounted on a smaller Saturn IB rocket, *Apollo 1* was scheduled to be the first test flight for the newly built command module.

With liftoff arranged for late February 1967, the crew of Gus Grissom, Ed White, and Roger Chaffee (1935–1967) were sealed into the *Apollo 1* command module on January 27. For hours, the crew went down its checklist with mission control, trying to work through a poor radio connection.

> Suddenly, a frantic, garbled cry was heard in mission control— there was a fire in the capsule.

Crew on the launch tower tried to open the spacecraft's hatch, but within seconds the pressure inside ruptured the hull, throwing the men back. By the time the fire was out, the crew was dead.

credit: NASA

The tragedy caught NASA and the nation off guard. People were used to the successes of Mercury and Gemini—the loss of three astronauts was a crushing blow to both the space program and national pride. The race to the moon had taken its first lives.

An investigation later determined that bad wiring caused a spark inside the crew compartment during the test. In the all-oxygen atmosphere of the cabin, the fire engulfed the astronauts immediately. The command module's wiring would need to be redesigned, and a safer mixture of oxygen and nitrogen would be used in the cabin to lessen the risk of fire. These fixes would take time.

Some wondered if the mission to put a man on the moon was worth the risk, which was suddenly very real.

SOYUZ 1

With America in mourning, the Soviets had an opportunity to take back the lead of the Space Race after nearly two years on the ground. Soyuz was the next-generation spacecraft, designed to carry up to three cosmonauts on long journeys into space. Like Gemini, Soyuz could change its orbit and even dock with another spacecraft. But unlike Gemini, Soyuz was also meant to go to the moon.

BUILT TO LAST

The Soyuz ("Unity") spaceship, first flown in the 1960s, remains in service today. The newest versions take astronauts to and from the International Space Station, and also serve as lifeboats for the cosmonauts in case of emergency. You can take a closer look inside Soyuz here!

PS

🔍 inside Soyuz spacecraft

BLAST FACT

Soyuz 1 was supposed to rendezvous with the crew of *Soyuz 2*, but thunderstorms ended up canceling the second launch, possibly saving the lives of the crew.

Brezhnev, eager to reassert his country's lead in space, called on Vasily Mishin to follow in Korolev's footsteps and pull off something spectacular. Moscow wanted the first Soyuz flight to be a rendezvous in space with crews switching crafts for the return home.

> It was something the Americans had never tried, and would be another impressive first.

But there were serious problems. Only two of the first five unmanned Soyuz flights were successful, and engineers and cosmonauts alike kept discovering dangerous issues with the craft. Yuri Gagarin (1934–1968), Soviet hero and backup pilot for the flight, wrote a letter asking to delay the flight until the problems were fixed. Determined, Moscow ignored the warnings. Brezhnev was confident that the issues would be overcome.

On April 23, 1967, *Soyuz 1* lifted off with cosmonaut Vladimir Komarov onboard. Right away, there were problems. One of the craft's solar panels failed, leaving it short on electrical power. Communication between the ground and Komarov was plagued with static. The automatic stabilization system failed. After just 18 orbits, the decision was made to bring Komarov home early.

But the problems didn't end. Once the spacecraft had slowed after reentry, the main parachute failed to open. As the capsule plummeted, Komarov activated the reserve chute, but that failed, too. When the landing rockets didn't fire, *Soyuz 1* hit the ground at nearly 100 miles per hour. When rescue teams arrived, the landing rockets suddenly roared to life as the capsule lay on the ground. By the time the fire was out, Komarov was dead.

The death of Komarov was a terrible disaster and a reminder of just how difficult spaceflight could be. The Soviets, too, had become used to success. Now, both nations needed to recover from their tragedies. The moon seemed farther away than ever.

A DEEPENING WAR

On the lunar new year of January 30, 1968, North Vietnamese troops launched a surprise, nationwide attack on South Vietnam. Guerrilla fighters attacked the U.S. embassy in Saigon, killing many. U.S. and South Vietnamese combat troops managed to fend off the offensive, but the loss of American lives brought stronger calls for an end to the United States' involvement in Vietnam.

With confidence in his administration severely damaged, Lyndon B. Johnson decided not to run for reelection and to instead focus on fighting a war that seemed to have no end in sight. More than half a million American soldiers were already fighting alongside the South Vietnamese, and more were on the way. Soviet and Chinese officials continued to issue warnings to the United States, cautioning that the war could grow larger.

Both nations hoped that a return to space could provide the world with some relief from the realities on Earth.

That summer, the Soviets faced their own struggles on the world stage. On August 20, forces led by the Soviet military invaded Czechoslovakia to stop the country from reforming its government and economy. This crackdown in Eastern Europe spread fear of Soviet aggression throughout the West, and a planned summit between the United States and the USSR was canceled. Already stuck in an unpopular war in Vietnam, the United States could only condemn the Soviet Union's actions.

AROUND THE MOON

Despite the Apollo and Soyuz disasters, the United States and the Soviet Union continued testing their spacecraft with unmanned flights as the race to the moon heated up. On November 9, 1967, the first all-up flight of the Saturn V lifted off from launch pad 39A with an earth-shaking roar and splashed down in the Pacific Ocean almost nine hours later.

The *Apollo 4* mission was a huge success, and von Braun's giant moon rocket was no longer a dream.

Not to be outdone, the Soviets responded to the Americans with the launch of *Zond 4* on March 2, 1968. The slimmed-down Soyuz capsule flew 186,000 miles from Earth, three quarters of the distance to the moon, before it self-destructed during reentry.

Just a month later, a second Saturn V flight was less successful than the first when *Apollo 6* experienced engine problems on its second and third stages. But despite its trouble, the rocket was able to complete its mission and was considered a success. The risky all-up testing had saved NASA a lot of time and effort, but nobody was certain if it would be enough to win the race.

On September 2, *Zond 5* carried a collection of tortoises and other creatures on a flight around the moon and returned them to Earth with a splashdown in the Indian Ocean. It was another impressive feat by the Soviets, and the United States feared that the next launch from Kazakhstan might carry cosmonauts on a trip around the moon before NASA could even put a crew into orbit.

(PS) Watch an ABC News report of the invasion of Czechoslovakia here.

ABC 1968 Czechoslovakia

SIGNING UP

In July 1968, a treaty to stop the spread of nuclear weapons was opened for signatures. The result of years of negotiations, the Non-Proliferation Treaty called for the peaceful use of nuclear energy and the commitment to reduce the number of nuclear weapons on Earth and eventually eliminate them. Among the first to sign were the United States and Soviet Union. Today, 190 nations have signed the treaty.

A scene from the first live television transmission from space

credit: NASA

RETURN TO FLIGHT

To a national sigh of relief, *Apollo 7* rocketed into orbit on October 11, 1968, with astronauts Wally Schirra, Donn Eisele (1930–1987) and Walt Cunningham (1932–) aboard. The smaller Saturn IB rocket was used to carry the redesigned command module, with plans to test the space-worthiness of the new craft in orbit. *Apollo 7* was the first manned flight since the Apollo and Soyuz tragedies, and any problems could mean even more delays.

The 10-day flight was packed with tests and experiments. The first flight of the command module meant exhaustive work to make sure the redesigned capsule worked properly.

Apollo 7's successful flight proved that the Apollo command module was ready.

While tests and maneuvers took up much of the crew's schedule, the astronauts still had time for a few television broadcasts.

NEAR MUTINY

Shortly after reaching orbit, Wally Schirra came down with a painful head cold that spread to his crew. The men became irritable due to the tight schedule and miserable feelings, and even ignored direct orders from mission control. Because they refused to follow orders, the *Apollo 7* crew never flew again.

Days after *Apollo 7*'s flight, the Soviets returned to crewed spaceflight with the launch of *Soyuz 3*. Once in orbit, cosmonaut Georgy Beregovoy (1921–1995) guided the redesigned craft to a rendezvous with *Soyuz 2*, its unmanned docking target. Unfortunately, he was unable to connect the two spacecraft, and had to call the mission off when his fuel ran low.

Two pieces were still missing from both programs: a lunar lander and the giant rocket that would send it to the moon.

A DARING PLAN

Apollo 7's command module test flight had gone so well that the next mission, *Apollo 8*, was set to test the craft that would carry astronauts to and from the surface of the moon. The lunar module was nothing like any other spacecraft before it. Unlike the streamlined capsules of Apollo or the smooth spheres of Soyuz, the lunar module looked like a large, awkward spider covered in aluminum foil.

With barely enough room for two, the lunar module was small and light, but it wasn't light enough. There were also problems with its ascent motor, the rocket that would carry the astronauts from the lunar surface back to the command module. If it wasn't ready in time for *Apollo 8*, it could put the entire program behind schedule.

After the Zond missions, the United States was worried that a Soviet manned mission around the moon was next. NASA came up with a brilliant plan. If the lunar module wasn't ready, *Apollo 8* would launch without it, giving engineers more time to work out the kinks. But *Apollo 8* wouldn't be a copy of *Apollo 7*'s flight. To beat the Soviets, *Apollo 8* would carry the first people to circle the moon.

APOLLO 8

When it was first planned, *Apollo 8* wasn't supposed to go to the moon. But the success of *Apollo 7* and the fear of a Soviet moonshot led to a daring and risky change in plans. You can learn more about it here!

PS

🔍 vintage space Apollo 8

MERRY CHRISTMAS!

On December 21, 1968, *Apollo 8* lifted off with Jim Lovell, Bill Anders (1933–), and Frank Borman, the first astronauts to ride atop a Saturn V. A perfect burn of their main engine set them on a course to the moon, and three days later, the crew entered lunar orbit.

As their spacecraft rounded the moon, the American astronauts were the first humans to see the Earth rise above the lunar surface.

The astronauts were celebrated as heroes. Millions across the globe were inspired by the flight, but for NASA, it was much more than an inspirational sightseeing trip. *Apollo 8* showed that the United States could send people to the moon and back— the only thing left was the landing and the small, spidery spacecraft needed to do it.

The mood on Earth and inside the *Apollo 8* capsule as it orbited the moon was joyous. No one had ever been so far from home.

Earthrise: The view from the moon

credit: NASA

After *Apollo 8's* incredible flight, the world waited for the Soviet's response, but the former leaders in the Space Race were strangely silent.

APOLLO 9

With the lunar module finally ready at the beginning of 1969, *Apollo 9's* crew of David Scott, Alan Bean (1932–), and Dick Gordon were assigned to put it through its paces in Earth's orbit. After liftoff on March 3, the astronauts tested the lunar module exhaustively. Stacked beneath the command module at launch, the lunar module had to be pulled from its protective covering, which was a difficult maneuver. The ascent and descent engines worked well, and the crew simulated the lunar module's return from the lunar surface and docking with the command module.

After more than a week of testing, the lunar module had passed all of its tests. With everything looking ready, the next mission would return to the moon with the lunar module in tow.

SO FAR AND SO CLOSE

The liftoff of *Apollo 10* on May 18 was the fourth successful launch in just seven months, an incredible achievement for such a complicated system. For the first time, all of the pieces of Apollo were traveling toward the moon. Color television broadcasts sent back spectacular pictures of the crew, the spacecraft, the earth, and the moon.

After safely entering lunar orbit, astronauts Thomas Stafford and Eugene Cernan left John Young behind and made their way toward the surface of the moon. At just less than 9 miles from the moon, Cernan stopped their descent over a future landing spot in the Sea of Tranquility before heading back to Young in the command module for their trip home.

BLAST FACT

Despite having all the equipment, *Apollo 10* would not have been able to land on the moon. For this trip, the lunar module had only enough fuel to approach the surface, not enough to land.

Apollo 10 had done everything short of actually landing men on the moon. The time for tests and rehearsals was over. The next scheduled mission, *Apollo 11*, would go for the finish line.

A MAN ON THE MOON

On July 16, 1969, a Saturn V carrying Neil Armstrong, Buzz Aldrin, and Mike Collins lifted off from the Kennedy Space Center in Cape Canaveral with the hopes and dreams of a nation riding along with them.

Once all systems checked out in orbit, the astronauts were off to the moon. After a three-day cruise to lunar orbit, Armstrong and Aldrin boarded the Eagle lunar module and began their descent to the surface. As they approached the landing site, computer alarms sounded. Despite the alarm sounding several more times, mission control in Houston, Texas, assured the astronauts that they could ignore it. They continued their descent.

As the landing site came in view, the astronauts discovered an issue. Large boulders dotted the area, making it too dangerous for the fragile lunar module to touch down. At just 1,000 feet above the boulders, Armstrong took over control from the landing computer. Carefully, he looked for a suitable place to set down, very aware that he had less than a minute of fuel remaining and even less if the landing was called off.

Finally, an opening appeared, and he piloted the Eagle module accordingly. Dust stirred up from the rocket motor obscured their view. The world waited. Armstrong spoke:

> "Tranquility base here.
> The Eagle has landed."

Experience the moon landing in real time with CBS coverage of the event at this website. How might it have felt to watch this as it was happening?

🔍 CBS coverage of *Apollo 11*

After checking the condition of the craft, Armstrong donned his suit and made his way from the hatch to the ladder. A television camera mounted on the outside of the landing module broadcast the moment when his boots first touched lunar soil. "That's one small step for a man, one giant leap for mankind," he said.[2]

A nation, and the world, rejoiced. More than half a billion people witnessed the event on television, with many more listening by radio. The entire world celebrated. For von Braun, it was the achievement of a lifelong dream, one he'd had since his days reading about rockets and spaceships as a boy in Germany.

Buzz Aldrin salutes the American flag on the moon

credit: NASA

After 21 hours on the surface, the first men on the moon returned to their tiny spacecraft to begin their return journey. They took with them samples from the lunar surface, and left behind several experiments, hundreds of boot prints, and the American flag.

THE END OF THE RACE

With Neil Armstrong's step, America crossed the finish line and won the Space Race. Six more missions to the moon would follow, and five would be successful. A total of 12 people walked on the moon, carrying out experiments, collecting samples, and even driving across the gray landscape in an lunar rover.

The Soviets had insisted to the world that they, too, would land on the moon, but it was not to be. Korolev's N-1 flew several more times, each flight ending in massive explosions. Every unsuccessful test was a costly blow, and the fourth and final explosion near the end of 1972 signaled the end of the N-1 and the Soviets' manned lunar program. Despite their disappointment at not making it to the moon, the Soviet cosmonauts congratulated the Americans for bravery and achievement. They knew just how difficult and dangerous the race had been.

The success of the program had many dreaming of even greater missions, perhaps with the cooperation of the Soviets. A lunar base and a mission to Mars were discussed. But after *Apollo 13*, with an onboard explosion that nearly resulted in more tragedy, interest in the lunar program declined. The expense was too great. Originally set to consist of missions to the moon, the *Apollo 18–20* missions were canceled. The cost of continuing to run a race after crossing the finish line was too great.

THE NEW SPACE RACE

While the early days of the Space Race were dominated by two opposing superpowers, private companies such as SpaceX and Blue Origin are making strides to make space travel more affordable and accessible in the future. You can learn more about them here.

 SpaceX

 Blue Origin

A historic handshake in space

credit: NASA

KEY QUESTIONS

- Why is the photograph of Earth rising over the moon such an iconic image? What does it mean to you?

- Do you think another exploration competition similar to the Space Race could happen today? Why or why not?

- What happens when politically divided countries find common interests in the sciences or arts? Can you think of examples of this today?

In 1975, the two former competitors performed a joint mission called the Apollo-Soyuz Test Project (ASTP). An Apollo command module and Soyuz spacecraft docked in orbit, with the crews shaking hands and exchanging gifts.

It was a strong statement of cooperation between the two countries after such a long and difficult race, but both nations went their separate ways after the mission. The United States focused on its reusable Space Shuttle while the Soviets assembled a number of small but highly successful space stations in Earth's orbit. The next collaboration wouldn't happen until 1994, when the Space Shuttle docked with the Russian Mir station.

Despite popular opinion, the Space Race was as much about the politics and posturing of the Cold War as it was humanity's drive to build and explore.

Without the competition between the two superpowers, it's possible that the incredible achievements in space exploration might have taken much longer to occur, if they happened at all.

Today's astronauts risk their lives for science and exploration more than national pride or to achieve a political goal. But the fact that they're able to do so is a direct result of the tensions and fears of the Cold War and the decisions made by those with more than pure exploration and scientific advancement on their minds.

Where would we be today if the Soviet Union and the United States had not faced off against each other in a competition of will, drive, and ambition?

RETURN ON INVESTMENT

For both the United States and the Soviet Union, the cost of the Space Race was immense. Billions of dollars were invested that some critics feel could have been better spent on Earth. Yet many important advancements, such as GPS navigation and satellite communication, were direct results of the space program.

- **Do some research on the costs of the space program.** What are your views on the cost of the space program? Was it worth the expense?

- **Compose your argument, and support it with facts.** Here are some questions to consider.

  - How did the Space Race harm or benefit each country?

  - If the Space Race had not taken place, where would we be now in terms of space exploration?

  - Now, take the opposite side. What are the opposing arguments?

> **To investigate more,** debate your argument with someone else. What are some of their points? How will you refute those points?

VOCAB LAB

Write down what you think each word means. What root words can you find to help you? What does the context of the word tell you?

collaboration, **GPS navigation**, **rover**, **simulate**, **space station**, **summit**, **superpower**, and **thrust**.

Compare your definitions with those of your friends or classmates. Did you all come up with the same meanings? Turn to the text and glossary if you need help.

WHAT IF?

The Space Race ended with a walk on the moon. What might have happened if the Soviet Union had won the race? What might have happened if the U.S. space program had continued to send people beyond Earth's orbit? Do some brainstorming and come up with some ideas!

- **Imagine the Soviet Union was the first country to land a man on the moon.** Write a short story that imagines characters and scenes in an alternative history in which the Soviet Union won the Space Race.

  - How would that have impacted the world?

  - How would the United States and the world have reacted?

  - How might the world we live in today be different?

- **Imagine that the Space Race didn't end with a walk on the moon and the United States kept the Apollo program going.** Research the Apollo missions that were never flown and find out about plans to travel to other planets. Write a short story that takes place during one of these imaginary missions.

  - How might these missions have changed the world?

  - What might have been discovered during these scientific explorations?

To investigate more, read a science fiction book that explores humans on other planets. What did the author imagine? Was it different from your own thoughts? How do fiction writers take factual information and use it to create stories?

A NEW KIND OF SPACE RACE

Private companies are now able to lift satellites into orbit and deliver supplies to the International Space Station—efforts once achievable only by wealthy and powerful governments.

- **Research at least two companies involved in private spaceflight, such as Virgin Galactic, Space X, and Blue Origin.** You can read about the three companies here.

  🔍 CNN billionaire space

- **Compare the companies.** What are their plans to put people and things into space?

- **Putting people and things into space is expensive and dangerous.** Do you feel that private companies can handle the challenges of spaceflight? Why or why not?

- **Some companies plan to take paying customers into space.** Would you take a ride on a private rocket?

> **To investigate more,** consider whether the danger and cost of space exploration is worth it. Compare your answer with others.

Today, the International Space Station, or ISS, is an example of peaceful cooperation in space. Fifteen nations—including the United States and Russia—helped design and build the outpost to perform experiments and study how spaceflight affects the human body. You can learn more about the ISS here.

🔍 space station updates

GLOSSARY

abdicate: to give up or renounce one's position of power.

adversary: a rival, opponent, or enemy.

aeronautical engineer: a person who designs and tests aircraft.

airlock: in a spacecraft, two sets of doors that allow astronauts to move from a livable environment to space and back again without losing air.

altitude: the height of something above sea level.

annihilation: complete and total destruction.

Allied powers: the countries that fought together against Germany and the Axis powers during World War II, including Great Britain, the Soviet Union, and the United States.

ambitious: a strong determination to be successful.

amateur: someone who is not a professional.

anonymity: being unknown.

Apollo (1961–1972): America's third human spaceflight program, and the first to land humans on the moon.

aquanaut: an explorer who spends long periods of time living in pressurized dwellings beneath the surface of the ocean.

ascent: to rise through the air, the early part of a rocket's flight.

artificial satellite: a man-made object that orbits the earth, moon, or any other object.

assassinate: to kill a leader.

astronaut: a person trained for spaceflight.

atmosphere: the blanket of gases surrounding Earth.

atrocity: a horrible or cruel act.

atomic weapon: an extremely destructive weapon that uses the splitting of atoms to create an explosion.

aviator: a pilot.

Axis powers: the countries of Germany, Italy, and Japan, which fought against the Allies during World War II.

Baikonur Cosmodrome: the Soviet and now Russian launch facility located near Baikonur, Kazakhstan.

ballistic missile: a missile that is at first powered and guided but is then pulled by gravity to its target.

Bay of Pigs: the location of a failed, American-supported invasion of Cuba by Cubans living in the United States.

bends: a medical condition that happens when the body experiences a quick change in pressure and gases dissolved in blood begin to form bubbles. Also called decompression sickness.

Berlin Wall (1961–1989): a wall constructed by the USSR and East German military to separate West Berlin from East Berlin.

blacklist: to include someone on a list of people who are considered untrustworthy or not suitable.

blockade: a way to prevent people or things from entering or leaving a specific place.

blunt: to be straightforward or direct. Can also mean a dull or rounded object.

Russian Revolution: the overthrow of the Russian government in 1917 by communist revolutionaries led by Vladimir Lenin.

Bolshevik: a member of the Russian socialist party that favored a revolution to seize power in Russia for the purpose of setting up a workers' state.

broadcast: to transmit or communicate, usually by radio or television.

CapCom: stands for "capsule communicator," often another astronaut, who speaks to astronauts during their flights.

capitalism: an economy in which people, not the government, own the factories, ships, and land used in the production and distribution of goods.

carbon dioxide: a gas that people and animals breathe out that can be dangerous if too much is breathed in.

celestial object: a star, planet, moon, or other object in space, such as an asteroid or comet.

centrifuge: a chamber that spins very quickly, creating a strong centrifugal force that pushes objects to the outside.

civilian: someone who is not a member of the military or police.

Central powers: a group of countries that fought against the Allies in WWI, including Germany, Austria-Hungary, Bulgaria, and the Ottoman Empire.

GLOSSARY

censorship: the suppression of speech or information by a person or group that finds the information or speech harmful.

chaos: a state of complete confusion.

citizen: a person who legally belongs to a country and has the rights and protection of that country.

Cold War: a rivalry between the Soviet Union and the United States that began after World War II.

collaboration: to work together, a group effort.

collective: done by people acting as a group.

command module: for Apollo, the spacecraft that carried astronauts to the moon and back.

communism: an economy in which the government owns everything used in the production and distribution of goods.

Communist Party: a political group that promotes the principles of communism.

constellation: a group of stars that form a recognizable shape or pattern.

controversial: an act or decision that is often disagreed with.

cooperate: to work toward the same goal.

cosmonaut: a Russian astronaut.

cult: great or excessive devotion or dedication to some person.

cult of personality: when a group uses propaganda to portray a leader as a hero and idol who can do no wrong.

de-escalation: a decrease in extent or scope.

decipher: to understand or solve something.

defect: to desert a cause or country to adopt another.

democracy: a system of government where the people choose who will represent and govern them.

denounce: to describe something or someone as wrong or evil.

deport: to send a foreigner away from a country.

descent: the way down.

dictator: a ruler with total control over a country, particularly one who has gotten that power through force.

diplomatic: to officially communicate between countries.

diverse: with many different people or things.

docking: when two spacecraft join together to temporarily form a larger structure.

ecstatic: overwhelming excitement or happiness.

eject: to suddenly be forced or thrown out from something.

endurance: the ability to last a long time.

engineering: the use of science, math, and creativity in the design and construction of things.

escalation: an increase in importance or seriousness.

exceptionalism: the belief that something is special or unique.

exile: to expel someone from their native country as a punishment.

Explorer 1: the first American satellite, launched on January 31, 1958.

fallout shelter: a shelter from the particles that fall after a nuclear explosion.

feats of engineering: the engineering or building of things that have never been done before.

fiction: stories that describe imaginary events and people.

fireworks: an explosive or burning device that creates a display of light and sound.

FLATs: members of the First Lady Astronaut Trainees, also known as the Mercury 13.

foreshadow: to hint or warn of something that will happen in the future.

friction: the rubbing of one object against another.

GPS navigation: Global Positioning System, a modern system of satellites that allows people to know their exact location on Earth.

g-force: a measure of the force of gravity.

Gemini (1961–1966): America's second human spaceflight program, able to carry two crew members at a time to Earth's orbit.

GLOSSARY

German-Soviet Nonaggression Pact: an agreement before the start of WWII between Nazi Germany and the Soviet Union stating that neither country would attack the other. It was broken by Germany in 1941.

gravitational pull: a force of nature that causes every mass, or object, to exert a force on every other object.

gravity: a force that pulls objects toward each other, and all objects to the earth.

Great Depression: a severe economic downturn during the 1920s and 1930s that started in the United States and spread to many countries.

guerrilla: a type of war where a small group of fighters uses ambushes and sabotage to fight a larger and stronger enemy.

gulag: a network of labor camps in the Soviet Union where people were sent as a punishment.

hatch: on a spacecraft, an opening or doorway through which astronauts or cosmonauts can travel safely between their spacecraft and space.

heatshield: an object designed to protect a spacecraft by either dissipating, reflecting, or absorbing the heat of reentry.

horizon: the point in the distance where the sky and the earth seem to meet.

House Un-American Activities Committee: a committee in the U.S. House of Representatives that investigated supposed communist activity during the early years of the Cold War.

ideology: a system of political or economical beliefs.

immoral: something that goes against what is generally accepted as moral, or right.

immigrant: a person who moves to a new country to live there permanently.

incinerate: to destroy by burning completely.

ingenious: a clever or inventive idea or solution.

invest: to put money, resources, or effort into something.

intercontinental ballistic missile (ICBM): a missile capable of reaching anywhere on Earth.

industrial: manufacturing, or building things, in factories.

Industrial Revolution: a period of time during the eighteenth and nineteenth centuries when large cities and factories began to replace small towns and farming.

International Geophysical Year (1957–1958): an international scientific effort to study Earth and space.

isolate: to be alone or separated from others.

Kármán Line: the boundary where the earth's atmosphere ends and space begins, 62 miles above the earth.

Kazakhstan: a former member of the USSR, now an independent country.

Korean War (1950–1953): a conflict between the Western-backed South Korea and the communist-backed North Korea.

Kremlin: in Moscow, the governing center of the Soviet Union.

labor camp: prison camps where people are kept in terrible conditions and used as slave labor. Also called concentration camps during WWII.

legacy: the lasting influence of a person or event.

Limited Test Ban Treaty (1963): a treaty that limited the types of nuclear weapons tests nations could perform, banning tests above ground, in the ocean, and in the atmosphere.

liquid-fueled rocket: a rocket that uses liquid propellants to create thrust.

loft: to propel an object up.

lunar module: for Apollo, the spacecraft that landed two astronauts on the lunar surface and returned them to the Command Module.

lunar: relating to a moon or a vehicle used to travel to a moon.

lunar orbit: when an object such as a satellite or spacecraft circles the moon.

mass: the amount of material that an object contains.

makeshift: a temporary or improvised solution.

maniacal: to have wild or unpredictable behavior.

Marxist: someone who supports or follows the theories of Karl Marx.

McCarthyism: the use of unproven claims against people, first used by U.S. Senator Joseph McCarthy against suspected communists.

Mercury (1958–1963): America's first human spaceflight program, carrying one person on sub-orbital and later orbital flights.

mesmerized: fascinated by.

miniscule: very small.

missile: an object or weapon that is propelled toward a target.

missile gap: a term used during the Cold War to describe a gap between the number and power of nuclear weapons between the USSR and United States.

mission control: where space missions are managed, monitored, and controlled.

moral: related to what is wrong or right behavior.

mourning: having deep sorrow for the loss of someone or something.

mutiny: refusing to obey orders or rebelling against authority.

N-1: a Soviet rocket designed to reach the moon. It never flew successfully.

NASA: National Aeronautics and Space Administration, the U.S. organization in charge of space exploration.

nationalism: an extreme form of patriotism.

nationalize: to give the central government of a nation control of all factories and agricultural land.

NATO: the North Atlantic Treaty Organization, a military alliance formed in 1949 between the United States and North American and Western European countries.

nausea: a feeling of needing to vomit.

navigation: finding directions for traveling using stars, maps, landmarks, or other methods.

non-proliferation: a decrease in the number of something, for example, nuclear weapons.

nuclear bomb: a powerful bomb fueled by the energy released from the splitting of atoms.

oppressive: harsh, unfair, or cruel treatment of others by a person or group in power.

Operation Paperclip: a program in which more than 1,600 German scientists, engineers, and technicians were recruited and brought from post-Nazi Germany to the United States for government employment.

orbit: the path of an object circling another object in space.

orient: to determine your position.

parachutist: someone who practices parachuting for fun or in competition.

paramilitary: an unofficial military force.

paranoia: a mistrust of people or things without a reason.

plague: to keep causing problems or trouble.

plasma: a form of matter that is similar to gas.

plummet: to fall sharply.

posturing: acting in a way to impress others.

premier: a head of government.

prestige: having or showing rank, success, or wealth.

primate: any member of a group of animals that includes humans, apes, and monkeys.

probe: a spaceship or satellite used to explore outer space.

promote: to support or encourage something.

propaganda: misleading information meant to build support for a cause or point of view.

prosperous: very successful.

propel: to push or move something in one direction.

psychologist: a scientist who studies the behavior and thought processes of the mind.

puppet regime: a government that is controlled by an outside person or group, usually another country.

purge: getting rid of people seen as disloyal or a threat.

R-7: a powerful, early Soviet ICBM that carried the first satellite and first person into space.

radar: a device that detects objects by bouncing radio waves off them and measuring how long it takes for the waves to return.

radiation: electromagnetic particles that impair human health.

radioactive: a substance made of atoms that gives off nuclear energy.

GLOSSARY

Red Scare: the fear in the United States that members of the Soviet Union or other communist sympathizers were plotting to overthrow the U.S. government.

Redstone: an early rocket designed by Wernher von Braun that carried the first U.S. satellite and the first American astronauts into space.

regime: the government in power.

rendezvous: to come together or meet.

retro-rocket: an additional rocket on a spacecraft used to slow it down.

revolution: an overthrow of an established government by the people governed.

rocket: a vehicle that turns solid or liquid fuels into a hot gas that propels the vehicle in one direction, usually up.

rover: a slow-moving vehicle used to explore planets.

rural: having to do with the countryside instead of a city or town.

ruthless: having no pity for other people.

sabotage: to secretly damage or destroy something on purpose.

saltpeter: a chemical compound used in fireworks, also called potassium nitrate.

satellite: an object that circles another object in space. Also a device that circles the earth and transmits information.

Saturn V: the largest and most powerful rocket to ever fly, which carried American astronauts to the moon.

science fiction: a story set in the future about contact with other worlds and imaginary science and technology.

sentry: someone assigned to watch or guard a person, place, or thing.

sexism: discrimination based on a person's sex or gender.

short circuit: a situation in which a current takes the path of least resistance. It may result in an electric shock.

Siberia: a large, northeastern area of Russia that is isolated and has a cold climate.

simulate: to imitate certain conditions for the purpose of testing or study.

sniper: someone who shoots from a long distance.

socialism: an economic and social system where the government owns or controls some businesses and resources.

solar system: the collection of eight planets and their moons in orbit around the sun, together with smaller bodies in the form of asteroids, meteoroids, comets, and dwarf planets.

solidarity: support within a group of people for an action, idea, or belief.

solid-fuel rocket: a rocket that burns a solid fuel to create thrust.

sounding rocket: a rocket used to obtain information about the earth's atmosphere.

Soviet Union: a communist country that existed from 1922 until 1991 that included present-day Russia.

Soyuz (1967–present): Soviet and later Russian spacecraft capable of carrying three passengers into Earth's orbit.

space adaptation syndrome: a condition of space travelers that feels like motion sickness.

Space Race: the competition between the United States and the Soviet Union to achieve the greatest accomplishments in space exploration.

space station: a large artificial satellite that can hold many people for long periods of time.

spacewalk: when a space traveler puts on a spacesuit and leaves the protection of his or her spacecraft to perform tasks.

spacecraft: a spaceship that explores the solar system and sends data back to Earth.

speculate: to make a guess or theory about something without having all the information.

Sputnik: the world's first artificial satellite, launched by the USSR on October 4, 1957. Means "traveling companion" in Russian.

stabilization: becoming less likely to move or change position.

stalemate: a contest where neither side is winning.

STEM: stands for science, technology, engineering, and mathematics.

steppe: a huge, generally flat, and treeless area.

streamlined: designed so that air or water can flow easily around something, such as an airplane or a shark.

strenuous: a physically or mentally difficult task.

suborbital: a path that takes an object into space but does not have enough speed to reach orbit.

sulfur: a chemical element often used in the creation of fireworks.

summit: a conference of high-level officials.

superiority: having an advantage over or being more powerful than someone or something.

superpower: a very powerful and influential nation, used especially with reference to the United States and the former Soviet Union during the Cold War.

surveillance: observing an enemy.

sympathizer: someone who agrees with an idea or opinion.

technology: the tools, methods, and systems used to solve a problem or do work.

The Communist Manifesto: a call for a revolution to form a collective form of government, called communism. Written by Karl Marx and Friedrich Engels in 1848.

thrust: a force that pushes an object forward.

totalitarian: a system of government that has absolute control over its people and requires them to be completely obedient.

treason: the act of betraying someone or something, usually your own country.

treaty: a formal agreement between countries.

tsar: a Russian ruler.

Tsar Bomba: the largest nuclear bomb ever tested, in 1961.

U-2: a high-altitude aircraft used for intelligence gathering since the late 1950s.

United Nations: a global organization where countries work together for the common good.

uprising: an act of resistance or rebellion against a person or group in charge.

USSR: Union of Soviet Socialist Republics, also known as the Soviet Union or Russia.

utopian: impossibly ideal.

V-2: also known as the "vengeance weapon," this was the first ballistic missile, first used in World War II by the German military.

vacuum: a space with nothing in it, not even air.

violation: the breaking of a law or agreement.

visionary: able to anticipate the future and see ways of doing things before many others do.

warhead: a weapon that is the explosive part of a missile.

Warsaw Pact: a military alliance formed in 1955 between the Soviet Union and Eastern European countries. It dissolved in 1991.

working class: people who work in factories and in jobs using their hands.

World War I (1914–1918): also known as "The Great War," this conflict was fought between the Allies (Russia, France, Great Britain, United States, and others) and the Central powers (Germany, Austro-Hungarian Empire, Ottoman Empire, and others), and won by the Allies.

World War II (1939–1945): also known as the Second World War, fought between the Allies (Great Britain, France, United States, Soviet Union, and others) and the Axis powers (Germany, Japan, Italy, and others), won by the Allies.

METRIC CONVERSIONS

Use this chart to find the metric equivalents to the English measurements in this activity. If you need to know a half measurement, divide by two. If you need to know twice the measurement, multiply by two.

ENGLISH	METRIC
1 inch	2.5 centimeters
1 foot	30.5 centimeters
1 yard	0.9 meter
1 mile	1.6 kilometers
1 pound	0.5 kilogram
1 teaspoon	5 milliliters
1 tablespoon	15 milliliters
1 cup	237 milliliters

RESOURCES

SOURCE NOTES

CHAPTER 1

1 smithsonianmag.com/arts-culture/wernher-von-brauns-v-2-rocket-12609128/

2 atomicheritage.org/history/bombings-hiroshima-and-nagasaki-1945

CHAPTER 2

1 trumanlibrary.org/teacher/berlin.htm and
nationalcoldwarexhibition.org/schools-colleges/national-curriculum/berlin-airlift/facts-figures.aspx

CHAPTER 3

1 *Into That Silent Sea: Trailblazers of the Space Era, 1961–1965*, page 67

2 *Into That Silent Sea: Trailblazers of the Space Era, 1961–1965*, page 64

3 Full speech transcript, also see clip listed below - jfklibrary.org
/Asset-Viewer/Archives/JFKPOF-034-030.aspx

CHAPTER 4

1 *Liberty Bell 7: The Suborbital Mercury Flight of Virgil I.* Grissom, page 175

2 *Into That Silent Sea: Trailblazers of the Space Era, 1961–1965*, page 113

CHAPTER 5

1 John F. Kennedy address, West Berlin, June 26 1963 - presidency.ucsb.edu/ws/?pid=9307

2 jfklibrary.org/Research/Research-Aids/JFK-Speeches/American-University_19630610.aspx
and jfklibrary.org/Asset-Viewer/BWC7I4C9QUmLG9J6I8oy8w.aspx

CHAPTER 6

1 *Space Race*, Deborah Cadbury, pages 255–259

2 Neil Armstrong, on the surface of the moon, July 20, 1969, *Space Race*, Deborah Cadbury, page 333

BOOKS

Ottaviani, Jim, Zander Cannon, and Kevin Cannon (illustrator). *T-Minus: The Race to the Moon.* Aladdin, 2009.

MUSEUMS

Smithsonian Nation Air and Space Museum, Washington, DC
airandspace.si.edu/learn/highlighted-topics/human-spaceflight

RESOURCES

WEBSITES

Vintage Space
youtube.com/channel/UCw95T_TgbGHhTml4xZ9ylqg

The Last Mission to the Moon (You can follow along in real-time with the final mission to land on the moon.)
Apollo17.org

NASA Spaceflight History
spaceflight.nasa.gov/history

Royal Air Force Museum
nationalcoldwarexhibition.org/schools-colleges/national-curriculum/space-race

QR CODE GLOSSARY

page 3: youtube.com/watch?v=kmqK7y4DyAs

page 7: nasa.gov/mp3/191322main_sputnik-beep.mp3

page 13: youtube.com/watch?v=JpVv49v8BLQ

page 18: ushistory.org/us/51f.asp

page 26: youtube.com/watch?v=5QuSXZTo3Uo

page 28: history.com/topics/cold-war/joseph-mccarthy/speeches/army-mccarthy-hearings

page 29: npr.org/templates/story/story.php?storyId=104578202

page 29: youtube.com/watch?v=TOSIM7RKn1c

page 33: youtube.com/watch?v=qdQHuiV_9AI

page 36: pbs.org/newshour/world/these-soviet-propaganda-posters-meant-to-evoke-heroism-pride

page 36: youtube.com/watch?v=jETJt_zbnKk

page 46: youtube.com/watch?v=FXj5lc_QUOM

page 46: youtube.com/watch?v=S2w8cWFE1Lk

page 46: youtube.com/watch?v=VZ_FHy6nGXA

page 48: youtube.com/watch?v=ZYucEQFYNf0

page 50: youtube.com/watch?v=3xd9kg-fJ9g

page 52: youtube.com/watch?v=TUXuV7XbZvU

page 54: youtube.com/watch?v=fv7LW0MljlI

page 60: the-berlin-wall.com/videos/first-anniversary-of-the-wall-541

page 61: youtube.com/watch?v=IKqXu-5jw60

page 66: c-span.org/video/?308689-1/president-kennedys-cuban-missile-crisis-oval-office-address

page 67: npr.org/2012/10/22/163395079/childhood-memories-of-the-cuban-missile-crisis

page 71: popsci.com/why-did-mercury-13-astronauts-never-fly-in-space

page 75: youtube.com/watch?v=2Ha9GJwlus8

page 80: youtube.com/watch?v=e6JKLGi-3TI

page 82: youtube.com/watch?v=Z62z64-AyH0

page 94: youtube.com/watch?v=YfCws6c6_Tw

page 96: abcnews.go.com/Archives/video/aug-21-1968-ussr-invades-czechoslovakia-14172343

page 98: youtube.com/watch?v=3CnBQp0Ry9s

page 101: youtube.com/watch?v=E96EPhqT-ds

page 103: spacex.com

page 103: blueorigin.com

page 107: money.cnn.com/2017/04/04/technology/billionaire-space-race/index.html

page 107: nasa.gov/mission_pages/station/main/index.html

INDEX

A

activities (Inquire & Investigate)
  Background Checks, 22
  Communism, Socialism, and
    Capitalism Today, 21
  Compare and Contrast, 87
  The Edge of Disaster, 72
  First-Person Account, 8
  A New Kind of Space Race, 107
  Propaganda!, 36
  Return on Investment, 105
  Splat!, 54
  To the Moon!, 88
  What If?, 106
Aldrin, Buzz, ix, 86, 101, 102
Anders, Bill, 99
animals in space, vii, viii, 29–30,
  33, 34, 44, 48, 61, 96
Apollo program, ix, 86, 90,
  92–93, 96–104
Armstrong, Neil, ix, 2, 84, 101–103
astronauts
  cooperative/joint missions
    of, 75–76, 104, 107
  dangers for, ix, 39, 41,
    44–45, 54, 56, 57–58,
    80, 81, 84, 92–95, 103
  early space program, viii, 38–54
  meeting/docking in space,
    ix, 64–65, 70, 81, 82–83,
    84, 86, 94, 98, 100, 104
  moon circling/orbiting,
    ix, 96, 98–101
  moon landing, ix, 2, 101–103
  moon travel preparation,
    52–53, 56–71, 77–78,
    79–86, 90–101
  spacewalks by, ix, 79–80,
    82, 85, 86, 101, 103
Atlas missiles, 61
atomic bombs, vii, 18, 19, 20.
  See also nuclear weapons
Aurora 7, 63–64

B

Bay of Pigs, viii, 50
Bean, Alan, 100
Belyayev, Pavel, 79, 81
Beregovoy, Georgy, 98
Berlin division/Wall, vii,
  24–25, 60, 74–75
Bolshevik Revolution, vi, 10, 11–12
Borman, Frank, 82, 99
Brezhnev, Leonid, 78, 83, 94
Bykovsky, Valery, 70

C

Carpenter, Scott, 41, 63–64
Cernan, Eugene "Gene,"
  84–85, 100
Chaffee, Roger, ix, 92–93
Cold War
  beginning of, 24–35
  Berlin division/Wall in, vii,
    24–25, 60, 74–75
  communism as central issue
    of, vii, 10–20, 24–26, 28, 30,
    36, 50, 52–53, 60, 66, 71, 95
  Cuban Missile Crisis in,
    viii, 66–68, 72, 74, 78
  ICBMs in, vii, 26–28, 38, 39, 61
  Korean War in, vii, 27
  nuclear weapons in, ix, 26–28,
    32–33, 38, 60–61, 66–68,
    72, 74, 75, 76, 78, 96
  Space Race in (*see*
    Space Race)
  Vietnam War in, ix, 78–79, 95
Collins, Michael "Mike," 86, 101
communism
  Cold War era, vii, 10–20,
    24–26, 28, 30, 36, 50,
    52–53, 60, 66, 71, 95
  *The Communist
    Manifesto* on, 11
  definition and description of, 10
  rise of, 10–20

Conrad, Pete, 82, 86
Cooper, Gordon, 41, 68–69, 82
cosmonauts, viii–ix, 43–45,
  47–49, 52, 56, 59, 64–65,
  69–71, 77–78, 79–80, 81,
  83, 93–96, 98, 103–104
Cuba
  Bay of Pigs in, viii, 50
  Missile Crisis, viii,
    66–68, 72, 74, 78
Cunningham, Walt, 97

D

duck and cover, 60, 61

E

Eisele, Donn, 97
Eisenhower, Dwight D.,
  30–31, 34, 38, 46
Engels, Friedrich, 11
Explorer 1, vii, 34–35

F

Faget, Max, 41
Faith 7, 68–69
Feoktistov, Konstantin, 78
First Lady Astronaut Trainees
  (FLATs), 70, 71
Freedom 7, 50–52
Friendship 7, 61–63

G

Gagarin, Yuri, viii, 47–49, 94
Gemini program, ix, 69, 77,
  80–83, 84–86, 90, 91
Germany
  division of, vii, 24–25, 60, 74–75
  war and weapons in,
    vi, 5, 6, 15–18
Glenn, John, viii, 41, 46, 48, 61–63
Goddard, Robert, vi, 4
Gordon, Dick, 86, 100
Grissom, Gus, ix, 41, 57–58, 81, 92

INDEX

Space Race
  animals in space, vii, viii, 29–30,
    33, 34, 44, 48, 61, 96
  astronauts/cosmonauts in,
    viii–ix, 2, 38–54, 56–71,
    77–78, 79–86, 90–104
  Cold War driving. *See* Cold War
  cooperative/joint missions
    in, 75–76, 104, 107
  cost/expense of, 75, 103, 105
  dangers of space travel, ix, 29,
    34, 39, 41, 44–45, 54, 56, 57–
    58, 80, 81, 84, 92–95, 103
  definition of, 1
  end of, 103–104
  meeting/docking in space,
    ix, 64–65, 70, 81, 82–83,
    84, 86, 94, 98, 100, 104
  moon travel/landing in, 2, 52–
    53, 56–71, 74–88, 90–104
  origins/beginning of, 1–7, 31–32
  popularizing space
    in, 3–4, 28–29
  rockets in. *See* rockets
  satellites in, vii–viii, 6,
    7, 31–35, 38
  science in, 63–64, 66, 68, 82, 90
  spacewalks in, ix, 79–80,
    82, 85, 86, 101, 103
  timeline of, vi–ix
Space Shuttle, 104
Sputnik, vii, 6, 7, 32–34, 38
Stafford, Thomas "Tom,"
  82–83, 84, 100
Stalin, Joseph, vi, vii, 13–14,
  15, 18, 20, 24–25, 30, 36

T

Tereshkova, Valentina, viii, 70–71
timeline, vi–ix
Titov, Gherman, 59
Tsiolkovsky, Konstantin, 3, 18

U

U-2 spy planes, viii, 45–46, 66
United States
  anti-communism in, vi, vii,
    14, 28, 30, 52–53, 66
  astronauts from, viii–ix,
    2, 38–42, 44–47, 48,
    50–53, 56–58, 61–64,
    65–66, 68–71, 77, 80–83,
    84–86, 90–93, 96–104
  Cold War with. *See* Cold War
  nuclear weapons of, vii, ix, 18,
    19, 26–28, 61, 75, 76, 96
  rockets/rocket development in,
    vi, vii, 4, 5, 6, 17–18, 26–30,
    34–35, 38–39, 52, 53, 90–91
  satellite launches by, vii–
    viii, 31–32, 34–35
  Space Race with. *See*
    Space Race.
  Vietnam War role of,
    ix, 78–79, 95
  World War II role of, vi–vii,
    15, 17–18, 19, 20

V

V-2 rockets, vi, vii, 5,
  16–18, 19, 26–27
Vanguard, Project, viii, 31–32, 34
Vietnam War, ix, 78–79, 95
von Braun, Wernher, vii, 5, 6,
  16–18, 22, 26, 28–32, 34–35,
  39, 44, 48, 53, 91, 102
Voskhod program, ix, 77–78, 79–80
Vostok program, 43–46, 48–49,
  52, 59, 64–65, 69–71, 77–78

W

White, Ed, ix, 81–82, 92
women in space, viii, 43, 70–71
World War II, vi–vii, 5, 14–20

Y

Yegorov, Boris, 78
Young, John, 81, 86, 100

Z

Zond program, 96